MIDWESTERN STRANGE

Midwestern Strange

HUNTING MONSTERS, MARTIANS, AND THE WEIRD IN FLYOVER COUNTRY

B.J. HOLLARS

UNIVERSITY OF NEBRASKA PRESS
Lincoln

Library of Congress Cataloging-in-Publication Data
Names: Hollars, B.J., author.
Title: Midwestern strange: hunting
monsters, Martians, and the weird in
flyover country / B.J. Hollars.
Description: Lincoln: University of Nebraska Press,
[2019] | Includes bibliographical references.
Identifiers: LCCN 2019005272
ISBN 9781496215604 (pbk: alk. paper)
ISBN 9781496216823 (epub)
ISBN 9781496216830 (mobi)
ISBN 9781496216847 (pdf)
Subjects: LCSH: Unidentified flying objects—
Sightings and encounters—Middle West. |
Extraterrestrial beings—Middle West.
Classification: LCC TL789.4 .H649 2019 |
DDC 001.940977—dc23
LC record available at https://lccn.loc.gov/2019005272

Set in Miller by Mikala R. Kolander.
Designed by N. Putens.

For Henry and Eleanor,
whose wide-eyed curiosity
inspired my own.

The most beautiful thing we can experience is the mysterious. It is the source of all true art and beauty.

ALBERT EINSTEIN

CONTENTS

ILLUSTRATIONS

ACKNOWLEDGMENTS

I am indebted to so many for so much. Most notably, the many folks who shared their insights and expertise with me so that I might get a better sense of the strange myself. These folks include Dr. A. R. Underwood, Linda Godfrey, Joe Schackelman, Jess Lamb, John Gutowski, Chuck Mathieu, Chuck Jones, Terry Doran, Miles Wilson, Lon Strickler, Jeff Wamsley, Colyn Carter, Jerome Clark, Lloyd "Mike" Isley, Bill McNeff, Thomas Tulien, Val Johnson, Jerry Shidell, Kurt Kortenhof, Tom Biasi, Pat Reinders, Lynne Rice, Mel Conrad, Dr. David Sprunger, Janell Hagen Samuelson, and many more. Thank you for your patience, your kindness, and your time.

Thanks, as always, to my inspiring students both past and present— all of whom demand I practice the same critical thinking skills I ask of them. Special thanks, too, to graduate student assistant, Jodie Arnold, whose interest in the strange matches my own.

Thanks to my colleagues and friends at the University of Wisconsin– Eau Claire as well: Chancellor James Schmidt, Provost Patricia Kleine, President Kimera Way, Dean Rodd Freitag, Dean Carmen Manning, Chair Erica Benson, Jon Loomis, Allyson Loomis, Molly Patterson, Nick Butler, John Hildebrand, Max Garland, Bruce Taylor, Greg Kocken, Dr. Justin Patchin, Dr. Jason Spraitz, Dr. Paul Thomas, Dr. James Rybicki, Dr. Jeff DeGrave, and Joanne Erickson.

Thanks to Dr. Karen Havholm and the Office of Research and Sponsored Programs at the University of Wisconsin–Eau Claire, whose sabbatical program proved vital to this project. Thanks, too, for the support provided by the University of Wisconsin–Eau Claire Academic Affairs Professional Development Program.

Thank you to the Wait! What? Writers—my aces in the hole.

And let's not forget Steve Dayton, Stacey Dayton, and Emily Kubley—heroes through and through.

And to the University of Nebraska Press, and in particular, Alicia Christensen.

Last but not least, to my family—who puts up with the strangest creature of all: me. Thanks for joining me in this search for truth.

AUTHOR'S NOTE

What you are about to read is true. Or as true as stories ever are.

I have confirmed what I can in the written record, though in a subject as strange as the strange, written records only ever get us so far. Due to this limitation, many of the "case files" included herein are heavily reliant on witness testimony, which you can believe or dismiss as you see fit.

For purposes of clarity, on rare occasion, quotations from interviewees have been utilized in a nonlinear fashion and with minor adjustments. In all instances, I made certain that the interviewee's meaning remained intact.

MIDWESTERN STRANGE

PROLOGUE

My Year of Living Strangely

Of the many items that have found their way into my basement's cabinet of curiosities, perhaps my most beloved is a Bigfoot sketch drawn for me by a friend. There he is tromping through the underbrush: arms swinging, gaze fixed, his trailing footprints the only evidence of his being there.

Each day as I sit down to write, that Bigfoot sketch remains squarely in my field of vision: a reminder of my first, true cryptozoological love. We first met when I was eight years old, a spry young man with a library card and a mother who trusted him to use it. While cruising the collections one day, I came upon him. No, not loitering in the romance section, but within the books themselves, sharing shelf space alongside dozens of other books dedicated to creatures whose existences were equally in question.

Enter the Loch Ness Monster, the Yeti, among a much larger cast of characters, all of whom I'd have invited to my birthday party had I thought they might attend. These creatures soon consumed my child-hood. While most kids my age asked Santa for dolls or toy trains, I asked for plaster of paris. You know, in case I had to cast a Bigfoot print.

After carting most of that library shelf home with me, I did what any monster-loving eight-year-old does: I founded the Indiana Monster Research Center in the storage closet adjacent to my bedroom. There, amid stacks of dust-covered photo albums and wooden tennis racquets,

I waited patiently for the phone to ring. After three days, our funding was cut (read: my mother needed her phone back), and so, amid public outcry (my own) the research center shuttered for good.

Down but not out, I tried a new tack: laced my boots, packed my backpack tight, and ventured into the "field." By which I mean my backyard.

Metaphorically speaking, I've never quite left it. Even today, every walk in the woods doubles as a Bigfoot hunt, and every swim in a lake leaves me scanning the surface for scales.

It's not that I'm obsessed, I assure friends and family, *I'm just open-minded.*

Yes, they smile politely. *You certainly are.*

Under other circumstances, such an open-minded sense of curiosity might seem a virtue, though rarely when the subject involves the strange. I've found this to be true of the general public, and doubly true of the academy—the professional world I inhabit. We in academia simply have little patience for the weird: get with the facts and spare us the speculation. I understand the sentiment, particularly amid a backdrop in which facts are often spun into anything but. The irony is that much of the research conducted by cryptozoologists, UFOlogists, anomalists, paranormal investigators, and the like undergo the same processes employed within academia's hallowed halls—namely, hypothesizing and theorizing toward a greater understanding of truth. Sometimes it's a scientific truth, other times a philosophical one. Things become sticky when we try to find truth in the in-between. Though to my mind, this is precisely the space where truth thrives, somewhere between the "evidence" and our perception of that evidence.

The savvy scholar knows better than to spend too much time on such tomfoolery. When dealing with the strange, we are safest when we draw the fewest conclusions. It's in our best interest to employ skepticism as a shield. To quote others. To bury our work in bibliography. And above all, to place an asterisk beside any claim that comes with even the slightest whiff of controversy.

You will find no asterisks here. Not because I've deduced the answers, but because this book isn't about answers. It's about learning to live in the questions—even when doing so offers a less-than-hospitable terrain.

*

What is it about the unknown that proves so tantalizing?

Perhaps it has something to do with living in a world with no shortage of answers. We are, after all, always just a search engine away from one so-called truth or another. But what happens when we extend our search beyond the confines of a search engine? What happens when we hit the road, crack the books, and listen to people whose voices are often muted?

This is a story of hitting that road, cracking those books, and learning to listen. It's a story, too, about spending a year amid the strangest tales the Midwest has to offer. And not just to be fascinated by them, but to explore the curious nature of our fascination, too. I'll be the first to admit that I've occasionally waded too deep into subjects pertaining to the strange. They have a way of sucking us in, and only the luckiest among us are spit back out where we started.

Which makes me unlucky, I suppose, because I'm not even close to where I began.

Though perhaps that's a good thing, too.

As a result of my journeys, I'm now compelled to view the world differently. To spend more time nodding my head than rolling my eyes, more time asking questions than answering them. These days I pay closer attention to all I don't know rather than default to what I do. The culmination of which has led me toward a new—and occasionally discomforting—way of living. One with intellectual humility at its core.

I've selected the Midwest as my testing ground because as a midwesterner, I'm well-versed in our region's oddities. And I'm well aware, too, that most people aren't. We Middle Americans have grown accustomed to being overlooked, which is precisely why outsiders ought to look a bit closer. The West Coast has its Bigfoot and the East Coast has its Champy, but what—beyond hot dish—could the Midwest possibly provide?

Trust me, the Midwest is just as murky and mysterious as the next place. Perhaps more so given the limited airtime our stories receive. When was the last time you cozied up around the campfire to tell of Joe Simonton's space pancakes or the Beast of Bray Road? When did you last share the story of Oscar the Giant Turtle or the horrible Hodag? Of the "Vikings'" fourteenth-century "discovery" of Minnesota? Or the potential role of Clam Lake, Wisconsin, in spurring World War III? Though the Midwest may be known as "flyover country," when we say "flyover," we mean flyovers by Martians and Mothmen.* As for our pastoral "amber waves of grain," well, you'll never guess what's lurking within them.

My search for the strange took me directly into this heartland: a week-by-week road trip spent crisscrossing the countryside. Quite purposefully, I struck out for the back roads and the watering holes found off the beaten path, anxious to hear the stories rarely recounted in the visitor centers. Admittedly, most of these stories were pretty weird and often hard to swallow. I swallowed them anyway, then spent months digesting what I'd been told. In the moments when I doubted the veracity of a tale, I took comfort in Daniel Webster's words: "There is nothing so powerful as truth, and often nothing so strange."

Strange as it is to admit, that's the one truth I know for certain.

*

This book began well before my yearlong smorgasbord of indulging in all things strange. It began in the spring of 2009, when I found myself at the helm of a composition classroom—a strange terrain, indeed, at least for a creative writing graduate student such as myself. I was twenty-five, and since I'd never taken a composition class before, I was shaky on the protocol—a trespass that quickly earned me the ire of my students. After demanding they write one too many persuasive essays, they returned fire.

"Why don't you?" they asked.

After a spirited debate—which I lost in short order—it was decided that I would, indeed, write a persuasive essay.

"And what shall I persuade you of?" I asked.

"The existence of Bigfoot," someone shouted from the back.

"No problem," I lied.

Weeks passed, my skepticism grew, and my persuasive essay began to reek of the same funk I'd warned my students against.

"According to *Webster's Dictionary*, Bigfoot is . . . umm . . . real?"

I wasn't fooling anyone. Even after consulting dozens of sources—everything from the International Institute for Species Exploration to *Harry and the Hendersons*—the most definitive conclusion I could reach was that Bigfoot may not *not* exist.

(Which, admittedly, was a long way from proving that he might.)

I'd cited my sources, paraphrased properly, but by essay's end, I'd still managed to fail my own rubric; mainly, by allowing unsubstantiated personal opinion to seep onto the page.

Only one line was remotely persuasive, and it had little to do with Bigfoot.

How are we to validate anything, I asked, *while remaining hell-bent on invalidation?*

This question soon spurred another, one which I've carried with me into the present day.

What if, rather than scoffing at the unknown, we approach it from a place of curious inquiry? What if, rather than dispensing with the strange, we try to embrace it instead?

It's harder than it sounds, particularly given my conditioning toward conventional wisdom. Throw in a werewolf, a Martian, and a multiverse or two, and things become even more complicated.

When I describe this project to friends, I'm often asked, "So are you Scully or Mulder?" Which, for those uninitiated with *X-Files*, is their way of asking if I'm the skeptic or the believer. With a well-timed chuckle and a shoulder shrug, I always dodge the question as gracefully as possible.

But I'm always left wondering: Is it possible to be both?

*

In the 1975 cult classic *The Mothman Prophecies*, journalist and UFOlogist John Keel wrote that paranormal phenomena are "so widespread, so diversified, and so sporadic yet so persistent that separating and studying any single element is not only a waste of time but also will automatically lead to the development of belief."

I appreciate Keel's warning not to waste time "studying any single element," though admittedly, that's precisely what I've done. Rather than glut myself on every news report on every phenomenon, I've opted for more modest-sized bites. By limiting myself to specific phenomena within a specific region, I give myself a fighting chance to better understand them. To do otherwise is to descend down a never-ending rabbit hole, one which—as more than a few folks have warned me—can be difficult to climb out of.

This warning hit closest to home when, in the midst of our phone conversation, a longtime UFOlogist who goes by the pseudonym Dr. A. R. Underwood informed me that his scholarly research on the UFO phenomena played a negative factor in both his professional and personal life.

"You ought to think awful hard," Underwood cautioned me, "before descending down a similar path."

As I am someone who enjoys his job and his marriage, Underwood's warning gave me pause. He was telling me, point-blank, that "the strange" was not something to be trifled with. As I was quick to learn, studying unexplained phenomena warrants the same rigor as any other subject. In fact, due to their tendencies toward obfuscation, perhaps they demand even more. Though I'm hardly equipped to give the subject its full due, I'm compelled to offer what I can. To turn over a few stones myself, particularly in an effort to better understand the human side of the strange.

Because as strange as unexplained phenomena can seem, none are half as strange as humankind's interest in them. To this end, rather than merely attempt to understand some of the Midwest's strangest stories, I've also tried to more fully understand the people who attempt to understand such strangeness themselves. Without exception, the people within these pages have proven to be thoughtful and serious-minded. Do I agree with their viewpoints? Not always. But that doesn't make me respect them any less. What I've found most admirable about the people I've interviewed—from paranormal experts and anomalists, to historians and eyewitnesses—is their refusal to shrug their shoulders when confronted by the unexplained. They've taught me that for as long as there have been mysteries, there have been people committed to solving them. A commitment that, as Dr. Underwood warned, all too often comes at a price.

The goal of this book is neither to debunk the mysteries of our world nor to confirm them. Rather, I hope to offer a closer examination of the stories themselves, and through them, learn more about why they fascinate us as individuals and society at-large. Each chapter is a "case file" because the majority of the "investigations" remain ongoing. I hope you'll forgive the lack of closure; I am hardly the first to fall short.

A secondary motive has long lingered within these pages as well—namely, establishing whether our grappling with such unanswerable subjects might fortify us against the onslaught of misinformation now embedded in our lives. By confronting monsters, Martians, and every strange thing in between, we challenge ourselves to look beyond our preconceived notions, to parse fact from fiction in an effort to come to our own thoughtful conclusions. My hope is that by lurching around in the muck for a while we might emerge—not with answers—but with a sharpened skill set to assist us in our shared search for truth.

"The answer is never the answer," Ken Kesey famously remarked. "What's really interesting is the mystery."

Believe me when I tell you that there is value in the not-knowing. That the mystery has merit, too.

Go ahead, take my hand. Let's wallow in the weird together.

---

* For the Midwest purists among us, yes, I recognize that West Virginia's Mothman sightings position it just beyond the Midwest's "official" boundaries. But given his proximity to the western Ohio border, I hope you'll allow me the stretch. If not, reader beware: there are plenty more stretches to come.

Part 1

MONSTERS

The oldest and strongest emotion of
mankind is fear, and the oldest and strongest
kind of fear is fear of the unknown.

H. P. LOVECRAFT

The Beast of Bray Road

1936–Present

NAME: THE BEAST OF BRAY ROAD

SCIENTIFIC NAME: DEFIES CLASSIFICATION

LOCATION: SOUTHEASTERN WISCONSIN

DESCRIPTION: APPROXIMATELY FIVE-FOOT-SEVEN, 150-POUND FRAME; HAIRY WITH A HUMANOID STATURE; OFTEN DESCRIBED AS AN "UPRIGHT CANINE," "BIPEDAL CANINE," OR A "DOGMAN." POTENTIALLY OF THE WEREWOLF FAMILY.

FIELD NOTES: SINCE THE 1930S, BEAST OF BRAY ROAD SIGHTINGS HAVE PERSISTED THROUGHOUT SOUTHEASTERN WISCONSIN (ELKHORN, DELAVAN, ETC.). IS IT A GRAY WOLF? A MUTATED CREATURE? A CANINE-SASQUATCH HYBRID? A MULTIDIMENSIONAL BEING? A WELL-TRAINED DOG WITH AN IMPOSSIBLY LONG LIFESPAN? WITNESSES AND EXPERTS OFFER NO SHORTAGE OF THEORIES.

WITNESS TESTIMONY: "IT WAS STOOPED OVER GORILLA-LIKE, HAIRY, AND WITH A TERRIBLE STENCH TO HIM. I THINK [MY FATHER] SAID IT SMELLED LIKE ROTTING MEAT." JOE SCHACKELMAN, 2017

CONCLUSION: UNSOLVED

Our story begins in the fall of 1989, when twenty-four-year-old bar manager Lori Endrizzi—having just finished her shift at The Jury Room—began the short drive back to her home. Along the way she spotted a strange shape kneeling alongside rural Bray Road in Elkhorn, Wisconsin. She slowed the car to get a better look, her eyes settling upon

Fig. 1. The Beast of Bray Road sketch. Courtesy of Linda Godfrey.

a pointy-eared creature with its back to her. As she drove forward, her headlights shone over its brownish-gray fur, revealing that the creature appeared to be feeding on roadkill. The creature turned, and for forty-five terrifying seconds, Lori stared at it, its fangs and wolf-like snout leaving an indelible impression on her.

"Its elbows were up, and its claws were facing out," Lori recounted to Elkhorn journalist Linda Godfrey. "I remember the long claws."

And she remembered the creature's estimated five-foot-seven, 150-pound frame as well, along with its hairy, humanoid stature. Though the creature was of human size, it hardly exhibited human behavior. What human, after all, feasts on roadkill at 1:30 in the morning?

Over the years Lori speculated on the creature's possible satanic nature ("It was just my feeling"), among other seemingly supernatural possibilities. "I don't really believe in werewolves, per se, but I believe something could be, well, conjured up," she told Godfrey, adding, too, that "if there were such a thing as a werewolf, this would be it."

The closest she came to identifying the creature came as a result of a trip to the local library, where, after a bit of sleuthing, she saw an illustration of a werewolf-like entity featured prominently in *The Golden Book of the Mysterious*.

"It was night, and it was quite late, but I know what I saw," Lori later confirmed.

And she wasn't alone in seeing it.

On Halloween night 1991, local resident Doris Gipson experienced a similar sighting.

She, too, was driving down Bray Road when her car unexpectedly slammed into something. Fearful she'd hit an animal, she pulled to the side of the road, exiting the vehicle to get a closer look.

"Here comes this *thing*," she told Godfrey, "and it's just running up at me! It was no dog; it was bigger than me!"

Judging by the pounding of its feet and the heaving of its chest, Doris remained convinced that the dog-like creature was running toward her on two legs. She ran too, leaping for the car door and driving away as the creature lunged toward the back end of her vehicle.

"I've never seen a human run like that," Doris remarked, "and my uncle was a track star."

Later that night, while picking up a friend from a party, she claimed to have seen it again, as did her passenger. Even with a second sighting, it was difficult for Doris to determine what exactly had crossed her path that night.

"I'd say it was a freak of nature," she concluded, "one of God's mistakes."

*

Nestled in southeastern Wisconsin's Walworth County, Elkhorn— population 9,975—seems an unlikely hotspot for strange phenomena. Yet for decades, its seven square miles have been home to an array of sightings, the Beast of Bray Road among them. On occasion, hairy bipeds (think: Bigfoot) have been spotted within the county limits as well, not to mention more than a few UFO sightings.

Leading me to wonder: What in the world is happening in Elkhorn?

Anxious to find out, one warm June day I fill the gas tank and make the three-and-a-half-hour drive from my home in Eau Claire to Elkhorn. But upon my arrival, all I find is a quaint, midwestern town that, at least on the surface, appears utterly lacking in anything strange. No Bigfoot, no UFOs, just tire swings and wishing wells and at least one front yard lined with decorative pink flamingoes. Out the driver-side window I spot the torso and legs of a man tinkering beneath his camper, while out the passenger side I glimpse a power walker, complete in wind suit, bustling past. Had I seen someone grilling hotdogs in the foreground of a Little League game, I'd have assumed I'd slipped into a Norman Rockwell painting. And my assumption was closer than I thought.

Though Rockwell never painted the town, New York–based artist Cecile Johnson did. In 1958 the Ford Motor Company dispatched Johnson to paint six Christmas scenes for the company magazine— five of which were later used as Christmas cards. Each of the artist's watercolors depicts wondrously midwestern scenes: one snow-blown landscape after another, each complete with a row of small-town shops, a moonlit barn, or the warm glow of a family decorating a tree. As a result of Johnson's work, sixty years later, Elkhorn remains known as "Christmas Card town." From a visitor's bureau perspective, it's a more enticing pitch than the alternative—Werewolf Town, U.S.A.

Though I've come to Elkhorn for the latter enticement, curious to learn more about the town's most famous creature from the woman who knows the beast best.

Author and Beast of Bray Road investigator Linda Godfrey meets me at Vasili's Corner Café in downtown Elkhorn at a few minutes before noon. For over a quarter century, the sixty-six-year-old has investigated all things "Bray Road," and through her efforts, has curated the world's best—and perhaps only—repository for information pertaining to the beast. Though she never intended to become the world expert on such a peculiar creature, fate intervened.

"One day I was a small-town wife, mom, and local newspaper reporter and cartoonist," she wrote in 2003's *The Beast of Bray Road*, "the next thing I knew I was fielding questions from media around the country about werewolves!"

It was a far cry from her art education training, though when the story struck in 1991, she knew she had to report on it. As Linda pointed out, it was the obvious thing to do given her local paper's motto: "Never Be Boring."

Throughout her decadelong stint at the paper, Linda strived to live up to that motto, though none of her investigative reports, columns, or editorial cartoons ever garnered the same attention as her Beast of Bray Road pieces. After publishing four or five updates—most of which ran in the early 1990s—it became apparent to Linda that the bipedal canine sightings she'd been gathering were hardly limited to Elkhorn.

"It was really a worldwide phenomenon," she says, leaning forward from her place across the booth. "People were reporting the same thing all over the place, and no one else was really paying attention or collecting these stories. So, I kind of became the go-to person inadvertently. I felt it was sort of my duty to keep these things for people, to be the keeper of the lore."

It's a sentiment I've heard often, particularly related to stories involving the strange. Historically, it's often seemed that there was more lore than keepers, though today, thanks to the internet, the world's many keepers have begun to bear the burden collectively by way of electronic information sharing. On the upside, such collaborations lead to a more inclusive and global information gathering effort; on the downside, it's impossible to vet the influx of information seeping into the virtual milieu.

For every serious-minded cryptid enthusiast, there's an attention-seeking hoaxer anxious to take advantage of the internet's porous gatekeeping. Semianonymous message boards serve as a breeding ground for such chaos, a virtual landscape run amok with a liberal use of caps lock and exclamation points.

Linda attempts to steer clear of this fray by offering a more research-driven approach to strange sightings, tempering each report with a healthy dose of skepticism. Over the past twenty-five years, Linda's online presence has continued to grow, her reputation buoyed by several book publications, including 2006's *Hunting the American Werewolf* featured in a 2008 episode of Animal Planet's *MonsterQuest*. No one is more surprised by Linda's transition from small-town reporter to leading expert on bipedal canines than Linda herself. Or leading expert on dogmen, if that's your preferred term. Or wolfmen. Or manwolves. I could go on.

Linda, for the record, prefers "unknown upright canine," though she concedes it's not nearly as sexy as "werewolf," which her publisher prefers. Yet for Linda, her work isn't about what's sexiest, it's about what's most accurate. Though "werewolf" is one way to talk about the Beast of Bray Road and its ilk, it's hardly the only way. And in some respects, such a term limits the more scientifically acceptable possibilities for what the Beast of Bray Road might be.

Yet ever since Lori Endrizzi's 1989 sighting, the term "werewolf" has continued to linger throughout Elkhorn. Perhaps beginning with Walworth County animal control officer, Jon Frederickson, who, at the height of the hullabaloo, famously scrawled the word "werewolf"

Fig. 2. Bray Road in Elkhorn, Wisconsin, home to many Beast of Bray Road sightings. Courtesy of the author.

on a manila folder filled with sighting reports which he kept in his office. Such a designation coming from a man in his position was all the confirmation many locals needed. Though Frederickson had used the term in jest, it's easy to forget that part of the story.

*

Our willingness to dispense with the facts in favor of the fiction is a phenomenon that extends well beyond Bray Road. Confirmation bias—that is, interpreting information in such a way as to confirm one's views—has been well-documented since the 1960s. If you wish to believe that the Beast of Bray Road is a werewolf, then simply steer toward the facts that make that outcome true. However, if you wish to believe otherwise, then steer in the opposite direction.

Trust me when I tell you I'm steering in the opposite direction. Yet for many, the prospect of a werewolf roaming the Wisconsin countryside is a little too good to overlook. To the believers' credit, in many respects the Beast of Bray Road is a perfect fit for our pop culture understanding of werewolves, particularly in terms of speed, power, and temperament. Most of all, the beast's humanoid qualities, most notably walking on two legs, further enhance the werewolf possibility—strange as it seems. But unlike Hollywood's version of the werewolf, the Beast of Bray Road hardly conforms to the full moon mythology, nor can it be warded off by a silver bullet.

Linda's the first to admit that she doesn't know what the creature is. Yet what's even more surprising is that "werewolf" isn't even the strangest of her theories.

"There's a category that I call the 'phantoms' or the 'bedroom invaders,'" Linda says, "because they're much more like the black phantom hounds from England."

My understanding of British-born phantom hounds is limited mostly to Sir Arthur Conan Doyle's *The Hound of the Baskervilles*. Americanized phantom hounds are said to behave similarly: supernaturally infused canines marauding the wilds and striking fear into all who lay eyes upon them.

As for "bedroom invaders," this refers to hounds who unexpectedly inhabit a witness's home. Not your average domesticated dog, but a tall, wolf-like creature with a long muzzle, sleek black fur, and pointy ears. Oftentimes, Linda informs me, the creature is said to resemble Anubis, the Egyptian god of the dead.

The possibilities grow even more peculiar from there: everything from variations of Bigfoot and Native American skin walkers, to a range of thought-to-be extinct prehistoric canines, including the *Amphicyon* ("ambiguous dog") to the *Borophagus* ("gluttonous eater").

Each possibility is intriguing in its own right, though each remains entirely speculative given the limited evidence at our disposal, most of which is anecdotal.

One possibility I've yet to discuss—perhaps the likeliest of all—is that the wolf-like creature seen wandering Bray Road is, in fact, a wolf. Gray wolves (known also as timber wolves) have occasionally been spotted throughout the region, and though their populations remain quite small (782–824 are believed to live state-wide), it's not impossible to imagine a few—if not a few packs—inhabiting the Elkhorn region.

According to the Wisconsin Department of Natural Resources (DNR), in the 1830s Wisconsin was a haven for wolves, somewhere between three thousand and five thousand calling the state home. But in response to wolf attacks on livestock, the 1865 state legislature took action: passing a five-dollar-per-pelt bounty and dramatically shrinking the population.

"By 1900, no timber wolves existed in the southern two-thirds of the state," notes the Wisconsin DNR.

Eighty years later, the wolf population teetered around fifteen. From 1985 to 2010 the population leapt to current levels. Much of this increase began in the early 1990s, when the Bray Road sightings peaked. The problem, though, is that relatively few wolves were sighted that far south.

And there's another problem, too, in claiming that the Beast of Bray Road is a gray wolf. Gray wolves—as well as every other variety—walk on four legs rather than two.

*

Maybe our story doesn't begin in the fall of 1989.

Maybe it actually begins on a cold, dark night in 1936, when thirty-three-year-old Mark Schackelman had his own encounter with an unknown upright canine just thirty-seven miles north of Bray Road. Schackelman, the night watchman for the St. Coletta School for Exceptional Children (previously called the St. Coletta Institute for Backward Children), was a God-fearing, former heavyweight boxer—one who never pulled pranks or punches.

Late one evening while walking the grounds behind the main building, Schackelman spotted a hairy animal digging frantically into a Native American burial mound, several of which lined the property. Schackelman froze, observed the hunched creature momentarily, then watched, astonished, as it leapt to two legs and vanished.

The following night, after a thorough examination of the claw marks on the mound, he returned to the site once more, this time wielding a heavy flashlight. As he approached the mound he spotted the creature a second time, all six plus feet of its furry frame standing brashly before him. The face-off continued for several seconds, Schackelman's flashlight beam scanning the creature's hands, claws, and dog-like muzzle and ears. The creature vocalized—three syllables that sounded like "gadara"—as he stood before the watchman.

Trembling, a terrified Schackelman instinctually turned to God, praying to be saved.

And he was. Inexplicably, the creature walked away.

On two legs.

At his wife's insistence, Schackelman never breathed a word about his encounter during her lifetime. Small towns talked, and she preferred the conversation not revolve around her husband having spotted some beast digging at a burial mound. It wasn't until several years after her death, when Schackelman himself was facing an uncertain medical situation, that he at last broke his silence to his son, Joe, nineteen at the time.

Mark Schackelman spent a Sunday afternoon in 1953 sharing every last detail with his son. A future editor for the *Labor Paper* in Kenosha, Joe put his budding reporter's skills to good use, reaching for pad and pencil and sketching what his father described.

"There were a lot of erasers," Joe tells me sixty-four years later.

At eighty-three, Joe Schackelman still remembers the many vivid details his father provided. Admittedly, it's an unbelievable story, though Joe confirms the veracity of his father's account.

"He was a very kind man," Joe reflects. "He didn't make up stories."

Instead, he kept his mouth shut for decades, though when he did talk, he offered a description slightly at odds with the Beast of Bray Road sightings soon to come. What Mark Schackelman saw seemed to steer the creature's taxonomy toward a better-known beast.

"It was stooped over gorilla-like," Joe tells me, "hairy, and with a terrible stench to him. I think he said it smelled like rotting meat."

You needn't be a cryptozoologist to offer the obvious alternative: that a terrible smelling, gorilla-like creature points us toward Bigfoot.

The "gorilla-like" description serves as the obvious clue, but so does the smell. Bigfoot, whose southeastern cousin is known as "the skunk ape," has a notoriously foul odor himself.

Which leads us to two equally impossible possibilities—Bigfoot vs. Werewolf—the convergence of which sounds like a B movie title that, by the end of this sentence, is surely in preproduction.

As for Mark Schackelman's take on what he saw?

"He may have referred to it as 'that damn thing,'" Joe recalls, adding, too, that his father remarked that it had come "straight from hell."

It's a lot to take in: the claws, the stench, the guttural utterance hurled forth from the burial mound. And frustratingly, none of it's verifiable beyond my secondhand source.

"How did you write about stories you couldn't confirm?" I ask the seasoned journalist.

Joe pauses, mulls it over.

"Well, I once tried a story on visitations with God, the Virgin Mary, that type of thing. And most of what I got I couldn't use," Joe admits. "I couldn't depend on probably 90 percent."

I sigh, nod, tell him I know how he feels.

*

Whether discussing the mundane or a monster sighting, it's hard to know who to trust. It's a problem I've confronted throughout this project, remaining open-minded to every possibility while tempering my open-mindedness with what I hope is a carefully calibrated bullshit detector.

Yet my detector's dwarfed by Linda Godfrey's, who's been busily sorting fact from fiction for years. When I ask how she knows who to trust, she tells me it all comes down to the witness.

"Those ten years at the newspaper were a very good training ground for me," Linda explains. "Every week I did one to three stories, and I'd be interviewing people, and when you talk to that many people for that many years you just sort of get a sense. Sometimes," she adds, "there are red flags."

And the best way to spot them is to meet the witnesses in person.

Given the limitations of time, space, and geography, this also proves impossible, but when it is possible—when a witness is just a drive away—Linda always makes the effort.

As my odometer will confirm, I always make the effort, too. If inter-viewees are going to lie to me, I prefer they do so to my face. Mostly because my bullshit detector works best at close range (body language tells its own story), but also because when you shake someone's hand and look into someone's eyes, deception becomes more difficult.

Though Linda's vetting process is equally extensive (in-person interviews if possible, multiple emails and phone calls if not), she acknowledges the potential for the occasional falsehood to slip past.

"Nobody's infallible," she concedes. And some stories just seem too good not to be true.

Raised in a strict Lutheran household, Linda grew up mesmerized by fantastical biblical stories involving arks, talking snakes, and people risen from the dead. And she was fascinated, too, by fairy tales.

"I was interested in all those things, and I remember wondering how some of these things could be, and how we could find out. If you think that way as a kid," she says, "you're probably going to carry that sense of fascination with you and want to explain it more completely."

For a quarter century, she's been doing just that, one sighting report at a time. Though Linda's the first to admit that it's difficult to gauge whether she's closing in on any definitive answers, unquestionably her collecting and curating of strange phenomena has provided a meaningful contribution to the subject at-large. Yet her contribution is complicated by her perilous positioning between the journalistic and speculative worlds. As I've learned myself, it's a difficult line to straddle, one that comes with a cost to one's credibility no matter how the story's spun.

When I ask about the importance of remaining open-minded on subjects such as these, Linda confirms that open-mindedness is vital—a prerequisite for any investigator. But open-mindedness only works when paired with pragmatism. To dispense with either attribute is to risk missing the truth altogether.

"I didn't originate this saying, but I think it's really true," Linda says. "'You should be open-minded, but not so open-minded that your brains fall out the back of your head.'"

I smile as she places her hands on the table and leans forward.

"If you don't care about these topics, that's fine. There's absolutely no reason why you have to. I don't have any agenda. But part of what I've wanted to communicate is that I do believe there is a reality that we can't perceive with our normal senses most of the time. And people's lives could be enriched if they were aware of them in a positive way."

I nod.

"So many people say, 'I won't believe it unless I can see it, feel it, smell it, touch it, hear it.' Okay, but what about ultrasound? What about all the light spectrum that is not visible to our eyes? What about electromagnetic fields?"

There are plenty of things that exist beyond our limited perception, she explains.

Why not the Beast of Bray Road?

*

Five minutes later, I'm sitting shotgun in Linda's Toyota Corolla. To the left is Elkhorn High School, to the right a trailer park, and just ahead of us, the sign I've been looking for: the one leading us to Bray Road.

"Now this is one of the most active areas," Linda says, nodding toward a patch of land around the road's first curve. "This is where the middle-aged couple saw it a few years ago. It ran out from that farm and crossed that field and jumped a fence line just like a hurdler."

I nod, feigning knowledge of this particular tale, though it's a new one to me. Many of them are. There are simply too many tales for me to keep track of, though Linda rattles them off with ease. It's her reward for a lifetime of study—a familiarity with the stories that few can match. Despite my efforts, I only ever see a fraction of the story. And the version I've built in my head is hardly the truest one.

Case in point: a tenth of a mile into our drive down Bray Road, I notice it's hardly the spooky lane I'd imagined. There are no gnarled branches, no darkened stretches, not even so much as a shadow. Aside from the occasional cluster of trees, all I see is farmland. No wolfmen, no dogmen, not even a farm dog snoozing on a front porch.

Perhaps sensing my disappointment, Linda reminds me of the many adjacent roads where other sightings have been reported over the years.

"There's no reason a creature like this would feel obligated to stick to one road," she says. "There are sightings on Bowers Road and Loveland Road and other roads around here. It's a territorial thing. It's not just *this* road."

She makes a good point. Why would a beast be beholden to a street sign?

As we reach the end of Bray Road, she says, "I'll make the loop around Bowers Road. Maybe we'll get lucky."

I nod, tilting my head to the floor mat to notice a tiny screen amid a wasp nest of wires tangled near my feet.

"You've got a dash cam," I say.

She nods. "That was my birthday present."

"So . . . you're still actively looking?"

"Heck ya," she says. "Other people are seeing it."

Taking my cue, I point my camera phone out the window, capturing the landscape as it blurs past. Yet I'm only a few snaps in when my phone informs me my storage is full.

Of course it is, I think, more certain than ever that the Beast of Bray Road will stroll past any moment.

After all, isn't that when mysterious creatures always appear? Just as the film runs out?

*

While perusing an estate sale in 2004 in Traverse City, Michigan, a man allegedly came upon a Super 8 film canister labeled "Gable Case #MPO41177–1" (later called the Gable Film). Curious, he purchased the reel, and upon viewing it, was astonished by what he saw: an instance when the film hadn't run out. The film came into the possession of radio personality Steve Cook, who soon released it to the world.

The three-and-a-half-minute clip features glimpses of what appears to be a seemingly normal wintry day from the 1970s: a snowmobile crisscrossing a wooded landscape, a man chopping wood, a German shepherd frolicking along an empty road.

Yet at around the three-minute mark, the "normal wintry day" becomes anything but. Suddenly the shaky handheld camera focuses on a large, dark creature in the distance. Seeming to have sensed the camera—or the human behind it—the quadruped charges, bounding through the sparse foliage until a brief glimpse of teeth and tongue fill the screen, at which point, the footage cuts out.

Despite the film's graininess—a hallmark of all hard-to-fathom footage—it was enough to make many believe. But believe what, exactly? That a werewolf-like creature had mauled a cameraman?

It couldn't be—could it?

Debate raged, soon to intensify further when a second clip was released, this one alleging to show the aftermath of the attack, including the cameraman's bloody torso.

Linda Godfrey and others were asked to examine the footage, most of whom agreed it was difficult to draw any definitive conclusions due to the quality of the film.

Yet on the 2010 season finale of *MonsterQuest*, the truth came out.

The creature captured on film was no creature at all, but amateur filmmaker Mike Agrusa. Donning a camouflaged ghillie suit typically worn by hunters and soldiers, Agrusa had created the footage.

For a moment, members of the cryptozoological world had wondered if they'd found their werewolf. But all they'd really found was what they'd so often found before: a carefully executed hoax.

"To become a hoax," writes Alex Boese in *The Museum of Hoaxes*, "a lie must have something extra. It must be somehow outrageous, ingenious, dramatic, or sensational. Most of all, it must command the attention of the public."

The Gable Film checks off all of these boxes. Not only was it successfully executed with drama in mind, but it commanded the public's attention by drawing upon a creature already of great interest: the werewolf. As a result, when viewers first watch the film, their subconscious has a ready-made explanation for what they're seeing.

After all, the Gable Film is hardly the first time we've seen a werewolf on film. And thanks to Hollywood, it won't be the last time either.

*

Late afternoon, once the roads run out, Linda and I call off the hunt. I'm hardly surprised that we didn't come across any wolves; frankly, it would have been far more surprising if we had.

After Linda and I bid our farewells, I head south toward the town of Sharon, Wisconsin—home to its own occasional wolf sighting.

Within minutes, I spot five of them.

I walk tentatively toward them, their muscles tightening as they watch me approach. They're not alone in their unease. Just a few dozen yards away I spot a skeptical white tiger as well, along with a couple of lionesses. And then, the most unlikely creature of all—a tiliger, a hybrid cross between a male tiger and a female liger, one of a handful anywhere in the world.

Days prior, I'd been astonished to learn that the town of sixteen hundred was home to such rare and wondrous creatures. Though my astonishment dissipated upon learning that the animals were all residents in the town's Valley of the Kings Sanctuary and Retreat.

I arrive at the animal sanctuary in the middle of a thunderstorm, honking my horn at the locked gate to make my presence known. Through the fog of my windshield, I watch as a woman in a yellow rain slicker marches dutifully through the rain to let me in.

My guide, Jess, welcomes me to the sanctuary, taking refuge alongside me beneath an overhang. After a few unsuccessful minutes of trying to wait out the storm, we hurl ourselves into it, walking from one chain link cage to the next as she introduces me to the big cats. En route, she recounts each animal's tragic tale: one bad circumstance or another that led each cat to the sanctuary.

As for the wolves, Jess explains as we walk toward them, they're actually wolf-dog hybrids: the result of breeders mating gray wolves with an assortment of large dog breeds—huskies, malamutes, and shepherds, among others.

"Previously people were allowed to own them, but then the DNR stepped in and made it illegal," Jess says, walking me toward one of the outdoor enclosures. "And since hybrids can't be released in the wild, they ended up here."

It's one of the few places they can go, she explains. Hybrids must be housed in a licensed facility, and since zoos don't generally want hybrids mixing with their wolf populations, options are often limited to sanctuaries such as theirs.

Drenched, Jess and I spend a few minutes observing the wolf-dog hybrids, watching them pace the edge of the fence, their eyes locked on my own. At one point the hybrid directly ahead of me lets loose a howl, immediately taking me back to every werewolf-inspired nightmare I've ever had.

To say the wolf-dog hybrids' behavior unsettles me is an understatement. It's not that I'm afraid I'm looking at a caged version of the Beast of Bray Road, I'm just uneasy for the usual reasons: the animals' superior strength, their rapt attention, their penetrating eyes.

"You know, hybrids are actually more dangerous than wolves," Jess says, adding further to my unease. "People think they're domesticated, but they're not."

"This is going to sound like a strange question," I say, "but . . . have you ever seen them walk on two legs?"

"Uh . . . no," Jess says, giving me a look that more than confirms the strangeness of my question. "The only time you'd see that is if they're jumping up on something or when they're fighting. Otherwise, no."

It's a response that makes it even more difficult to chalk up the beast to a gray wolf.

But if not that, I wonder, *then what?*

*

Linda's got a theory.

"I call it the indigenous dogman theory," she explained to me as we drove.

What people might be seeing on Bray Road, Linda suggested, are *mutated* wolves.

"It's not an outrageous mutation to occur," she said, referring to their bipedal nature, "and it would have some advantages in terms of being able to carry its prey around and see above the prairie grass at what's coming." Linda doesn't claim the mutation to be the result of hundreds of thousands of years of evolution, but simply a natural adaptation, one that's been passed on for decades.

"If it's a natural animal, it'd be long dead by now," she said. "I think the average lifespan for a wolf is like seven, eight, nine years, and it's been over twenty-five since I wrote the stories." She added, too, that if Mark Schackelman's 1936 sighting was a representative from the same family of creatures, then the timeline likely stretches back much further. Leaving her with but one conclusion: if the Beast of Bray Road is indeed flesh and blood, then it's been reproducing (and mutating) for decades.

But is a biological mutation really necessary to transition a wolf from four legs to two? Could it simply be a matter of training?

In 2014 a well-trained Pomeranian named Jiff claimed the title "Fastest Dog on Two Paws," taking home not one, but two world records: fastest ten meters on hind legs (just shy of seven seconds) and fastest five meters on front paws (just under eight seconds). While trained performance dogs can sustain bipedal motion for some time (a slew of viral videos confirms it), I've never heard of any wolves managing such a feat. The best proof I've seen of a noncanine quadruped excelling in the bipedal world was captured on a 2016 video from South Korea's Everland theme park. In it, a pair of bears run alongside a tourist bus and accept tips in the form of food. It's a scene straight out of *Yogi Bear*, minus the picnic basket. The video footage—so comical, so curious— reaches its climax when one bear casually places a paw atop the other's shoulder, regaining balance in a manner we humans practice, too.

But do I really think that trained performance wolves are honing their skills in and around Elkhorn, Wisconsin? Or that a couple of wolfish-looking bears have taken to two legs instead of four?

I do not.

But following an afternoon chatting with Linda about so many strange possibilities (from canine-Sasquatch hybrids to visitors from other dimensions), the notion that a familial line of canines might have simply mutated—or changed behavior—seems, if you'll forgive the pun, to have legs.

*

After a search nearly as extensive as trying to find the Beast of Bray Road, I at last track down a worn copy of *The Golden Book of the Mysterious*—the 1976 title that includes the werewolf illustration Lori Endrizzi felt matched what she'd seen in 1989. In the section titled "Werewolves and Vampires by Moonlight" I view the illustration for myself: a gray-furred, glowing-eyed wolf forever frozen in a crouch, his hands (not paws, mind you) gripped tight to the craggy rock before him.

Of the werewolf's many depictions, perhaps this is the most haunting. Though maybe, too, my interpretation's colored by the surprising language on the upper half of the page—a step-by-step guide to becoming a werewolf, oddly (and disconcertingly) specific for a children's book. Upon moving beyond the instructions (which include bathing "naked in the moonlight" and mixing a witch's brew with "the fat of young children"), my eyes return once more to the picture itself, complete with all its stylized charm.

I'm no stranger to such images; great swaths of my childhood were spent marveling at books much like this one: part pulp, part peculiarity. Perhaps the terror I felt upon seeing the *Golden Book*'s version of the werewolf had less to do with the creature itself and more to do with where that image transported me: not to Bray Road in Elkhorn, Wisconsin, but to Breconshire Drive in Fort Wayne, Indiana, where my imaginative early years were populated with all sorts of beasts. Many of whom—to my mind, at least—lived just a snout length away.

After indulging in a bit of enthusiastic page-flipping, I am surprised to learn that *The Golden Book of the Mysterious* offers more than a mere werewolf image, but commentary, too, related to the role mystery plays in our lives.

"Without curiosity and awe—the desire to learn about something strange or unknown combined with reverence and a tinge of fear— mankind would never have come down from the trees or out of the cave. In fact he never would have developed any civilization at all," authors Jane Werner Watson and Sol Chaneles posit.

Though I'm not sure I credit all of civilization to the power of mysteries, I do agree with their later take on what mysteries provide us: a one-way ticket on an introspective journey to view our world differently. In doing so, the authors conclude, we more fully understand "the magic of mystery—its power to open our eyes and minds, to stimulate our boundless curiosity."

Though, of course, one's "boundless curiosity" comes at a price.

As Linda and I wrapped up our lunch at Vasili's Corner Café, I'd asked her if most "serious-minded" journalists know better than to investigate strange phenomena.

"Oh yeah, definitely," Linda agreed, hardly skipping a beat. "You know, you get somebody starting journalism and they're thinking, 'Some day in the future there's a Pulitzer Prize in store for me, but will I get that writing about ghosts? No, probably not.' I think you have to have a certain interest in these subjects if you're going to risk writing something of this sort because it is a risk to many careers."

"Has this subject been a risk to yours?" I pressed.

"I'm not a scientist, so I have no scientific reputation to wreck. I think I said that in one of my books. When you're an artist people already think you're loony," she smiled.

Like Linda, what I lack in one field, I hope to make up in another. Thinking broadly about the world's oddities can transcend science, and when we bring in other subjects—philosophy, psychology, even literature and the arts—we can't help but stumble upon different answers. Not always the right ones, but perspectives and paradigms nonetheless worthy of our consideration. It's the difference between seeing the world through a panoramic lens rather than peeking through a keyhole. It's about thinking broadly and openly, while understanding, too, how skepticism can serve as a safeguard.

Linda knows this better than most. Which is why she keeps her dash cam at the ready, always prepared to gather proof that might lead her toward a conclusion. And it's why I keep my eyes wide as well, always hopeful for something to make me think differently.

Shortly before leaving Elkhorn, something does make me think differently.

The town motto, which reads: "Living in Harmony."

I shake my head as I drive out of town, wonder: *In harmony with what?*

CASE FILE #2

Oscar the Turtle

March 1949

NAME: OSCAR THE TURTLE, A.K.A. THE BEAST OF BUSCO

SCIENTIFIC NAME: *CHELYDRA SERPENTINA* (COMMON SNAPPING TURTLE)
   OR *MACROCHELYS TEMMINCKII* (ALLIGATOR SNAPPING TURTLE)

LOCATION: FULK LAKE IN CHURUBUSCO, INDIANA

DESCRIPTION: BETWEEN 250 AND 400 POUNDS; RAZOR-BEAKED, DEAD-EYED,
   AND WITH A SHELL ESTIMATED TO BE THE SIZE OF A DINING-ROOM TABLE.

FIELD NOTES: IN MARCH OF 1949, THE TOWN OF CHURUBUSCO, INDIANA,
   FOUND ITSELF CAUGHT UP IN A GIANT TURTLE HUNT. WHILE THE TUR-
   TLE WAS ALLEGED TO HAVE BEEN GLIMPSED BEFORE, FOR BETTER
   OR WORSE, IN THE SPRING OF 1949, THE REST OF THE WORLD TOOK
   NOTICE. NATIONAL JOURNALISTS DESCENDED UPON THE SMALL TOWN,
   PERHAPS SCARING OSCAR AWAY FOR GOOD, BUT SOLIDIFYING HIS
   LEGACY IN THE PROCESS.

WITNESS TESTIMONY: "WE SAW THE BIG WAVES A-ROLLING AND UP CAME
   THAT TURTLE. . . . I SAW THAT BIG HEAD STICKING UP AND THE WAVES
   GOING AWAY LIKE IT WAS A SUBMARINE." ORA BLUE, 1948

CONCLUSION: AFTER LOCAL FARMER GALE HARRIS'S MANY UNSUCCESS-
   FUL ATTEMPTS TO LURE OSCAR FROM THE MUDDY BOTTOMS OF FULK
   LAKE, THE TURTLE IS NO LONGER BELIEVED TO RESIDE THERE. BUT
   THERE ARE PLENTY OF OTHER NEARBY LAKES, OF COURSE . . .

Picture this: the biggest, meanest, most terrible turtle the Midwest
had ever seen.

Fig. 3. Gale Harris holding tight to a turtle (not Oscar) in Churubusco, Indiana, 1949. Courtesy of Churubusco Historical Society.

Or not seen.

Depending on who you ask.

Yet in March of 1949 there was little doubt to the people of Churu-busco, Indiana, that a creature of impossible proportions lurked in the waters of Fulk Lake, seven acres of muck and bog and swampland that descended ninety or so feet deep. Some argued it was an ideal habitat for a turtle of such magnitude—quiet, fish-filled, and far from prying eyes. Though a four-hundred-pound turtle could hardly stay hidden forever, and he didn't.

On Tuesday, July 27, 1948, local fishermen Ora Blue and Charlie Wilson encountered the giant turtle while casting their lines in the lake.

"We saw the big waves a-rolling and up came that turtle," reported Blue. "I saw that big head sticking up and the waves going away like it was a submarine."

As fish stories go, this was a particularly big one, and property owners Gale and Helen Harris were quick to dismiss the claim. Ora Blue (Gale Harris's brother-in-law) had a reputation for being a prankster, and alleging to have spotted a gargantuan turtle seemed like just the kind of prank he might pull.

Yet Gale Harris's doubts were put to rest the following March, when he and the Reverend Orville Reese spotted the beast themselves while repairing Harris's barn roof.

Curious about the strange shape burbling in the early morning water, Gale and Orville descended from the roof and scurried into the nearest rowboat, gripping tight to the oars as they paddled toward the ripples. Within minutes they'd reached their destination, at which point they peered into the water, waiting.

Gale Harris kept watch from one side of the boat, while Orville Reese watched from the other.

"Here it is over here," Orville called.

"No," Gale replied, "here it is over here."

Suddenly, they were struck by a terrible truth: they were staring at opposite sides of the same turtle.

His shell was as big as a dining-room table, six feet of mud-colored

Fig. 4. Oscar the Turtle likenesses can be seen throughout Churubusco, Indiana, including this street corner. Courtesy of the author.

bone plates wrapped tight around a meaty frame. Weighing in somewhere between 250 and 400 pounds (Oscar never tiptoed onto any scales), the creature was all teeth and neck and fury. An overgrown snapping turtle, perhaps, or an alligator snapper who'd found himself a long way from home. Both men knew the turtle beneath their boat was impossibly large, and yet, what other explanation was there? They'd seen what they'd seen, and they sure weren't going to keep it a secret.

In a town of Churubusco's size, news has a way of spreading like wildfire. While the weekly paper, the *Churubusco Truth*, served as one conduit to report the goings-on around the area, for a speedier update, citizens needed only to sidle up to a stool at the local café or watering hole. The close-knit community of twelve hundred made it its business to know everyone else's, though rarely had their "business" garnered the attention of the wider world.

That changed on March 7, 1949, when the Whitley County clerk penned an article for the local newspaper describing Gale and Orville's alleged turtle encounter. Word soon traveled fifteen miles south to the big city of Fort Wayne (population 120,000 or so), where twenty-three-year-old Laura Etz of the United Press scooped the story on a slow news day and sent it over the wires.

"That was probably in the afternoon," Etz recalled years later, "and the next morning when I came into the office there were urgent messages to me from the Chicago bureau: need new lede on Churubusco turtle."

Reporters and photographers hustled in from an array of wide-reaching publications, including *Life* magazine and the *Chicago Sun-Times*. Meanwhile, just a stone's throw away in Fort Wayne, the *News-Sentinel* took it upon itself to name the turtle Oscar, while the competing paper, the *Journal Gazette*, opted for the more alliterative "Beast of Busco" instead. For some readers, it seemed two names too many for a turtle whose existence remained in question. Yet not for Fort Wayne journalists, who were acutely aware of the importance of humanizing their subject—even if their subject was hardly human at all.

*

Today the town remains nearly as elusive as its monster. Tucked into less than a square mile of brick buildings (a diner, hardware store, auto repair shop, funeral home, etc.), Churubusco, Indiana, is a point on a map that often gets overlooked. Dr. John Gutowski, who in 1977 wrote his dissertation on the town and its turtle, described Churubusco as "a typical Midwestern, middle-American, Main Street town." Forty years later, the description still fits.

Within this typical midwestern town are typical midwestern people: wholesome, congenial, and hardworking. Gutowski noted that the Churubuscoan citizen "prefer[red] to regard both himself and others as if all were average Americans."

And for a while they achieved their averageness admirably. But by mid-March of 1949, the town and its people had become anything but. Like it or not, suddenly they were extraordinary, and as a result, Churubusco found itself faced with a problem they'd never encountered: traffic jams.

In response to the turtle-related news coverage, throngs of cars lined the gravel road leading toward Fulk Lake, an estimated three thousand visitors crowding onto the Harris property on March 14 alone. As a result of their uninvited four-legged guest, they were forced to deal with plenty of uninvited two-legged guests as well.

"We couldn't sit down and eat a meal in peace or get our work done on schedule," Helen Harris remarked twenty-five years later. For weeks, daily chores such as milking cows and washing dishes were interrupted by the press and the public, both of whom wanted to get as close to Oscar as they could, which meant getting close to the Harrises, too.

"We had no privacy in our home," Helen Harris continued. "People came by the hundreds and would walk right into the home without knocking."

For modest midwesterners such as the Harrises, their guests' behavior was nothing short of mind-boggling. Who were these people who barged onto their private residence, tearing down fences and trampling crops? And for what? A glimpse of a turtle?

Decades later, Helen Harris recalled just how quickly their turtle became their albatross.

"We were a happy, peaceful family of four," she said, "until Oscar became a part of our lives."

*

Forty years after the initial sightings, Oscar became a part of my life, too. I'd grown up a mere fifteen miles away in Fort Wayne, meaning by the time I turned five I knew to fear northern Indiana's murky lakes. Well into my teens I could often be found curling my toes around the edges of one dock or another, pausing—and sometimes praying—before taking that fateful leap. Where others saw nothing, I saw the dark and impenetrable water. And within it, an antediluvian monster, dead-eyed and licking his lips. I couldn't help but imagine that sharp-beaked creature awaiting my inelegant pencil dives, carefully camouflaged within his moss-covered shell to ensure he remained undetected. For me, he was the singular source of every unexplained burble in every otherwise placid lake. While my friends all believed their monsters lived under their beds, I knew mine lived just below the waterline.

Oscar was the stuff of nightmares, and after awakening to a few cold sweats, I began avoiding Churubusco altogether. Which, admittedly, was hardly a problem given that we never had much reason to go there anyway.

Decades later, Oscar lures me back, urging me to confirm (or deny) his existence once and for all. On a cool day in March I park the car and make my way inside the Churubusco History Center, a modest, one-room structure complete with a table and a couple of chairs. What the center lacks in flashy displays it makes up for in guys named Chuck. Two in total—sixty-seven-year-old Chuck Mathieu and seventy-six-year-old Chuck Jones—both of whom welcome me heartily and agree to tell me the town's tale.

"There's more here than just Oscar," Chuck Mathieu promises. And he's right. In the town's 170+ year history, there have also been a pair of fires, a bank robbery, and a tornado. Which is to say nothing of the generations of Churubuscoans who've lived meaningful lives in their beloved town, contributing to its culture and economy in countless ways. Though to the outside world, Churubusco remains mostly known for its turtle, a creature that—at least judging by the "Welcome to Turtle Town, U.S.A." sign that greeted me upon my arrival—the locals have more than embraced.

Even if I'd somehow missed the welcome sign, there's no missing the multitude of turtles that populate the streets. Oscar holds the unique honor of being everywhere and nowhere all at once. His cartoonish likeness populates signage and storefronts, though Oscar—the living, breathing version, that is—remains perpetually (and perhaps conveniently) hidden.

Thankfully, the Chucks are more than willing to fill me in on Oscar's story. Offering me a foldout chair, they take me on their guided tour of turtle lore, beginning with Oscar-related newspaper clippings, then moving me through decades' worth of paraphernalia from their annual Turtle Days festival.

Notably absent, however, is any definitive proof of Oscar's existence.
"Anything else?" I ask, peering hopefully around the room for some tossed aside giant turtle shell.

"Well," Chuck Mathieu says, "there's the net they used to try to capture him with."

"Net?" I ask, my eyebrow raised. "You've got the net?"

"Well not here," Mathieu clarifies. "Last I heard it was in the basement of the funeral home."

I make a note, promising to follow up soon.

Though hardly the smoking gun I'm after, it's better than nothing. In fact, barring an Oscar sighting, what better than a three-hundred-foot net to serve as tangible proof of the turtle's existence? Or at least Churubusco's commitment to its existence. While plenty of photos and rumors remain, it's the net that best epitomizes what I'm after: proof of a town ensnared by its own story.

And no one member of the town was more ensnared than Gale Harris.

Described as a "sober, upstanding farmer" by local newspapers and a "strict Nazarene Christian" by Gutowski, Gale Harris's squeaky-clean reputation became sullied in the spring of 1949. People smelled a hoax, or at least a wildly exaggerated tale. Despite Gale Harris's unwavering commitment to what he'd seen, nothing seemed to satisfy the doubters. Gale was aware that the best way to enhance his credibility was to disprove the naysayers, but he knew, too, that the only way to do so involved capturing the turtle—a task easier said than done.

Helen Harris, who had little interest in Oscar, was equally upset by the public's growing distrust of her family. In director Terry Doran's 1994 documentary *The Hunt for Oscar*, Helen confided that "the reason that I finally decided I would go along with [the turtle hunt] . . . was because the public thought it was just a publicity story, wasn't anything to it. Well, in my way of thinking, it was the same as calling us liars. . . . And I said, 'I don't care whether we get a penny out of it if we can just prove to people that we are telling the truth.'"

Initially, Gale Harris had hoped to at least get a few pennies out of it. And who could blame him? After all, a turtle of Oscar's proportions might've netted a sizable profit as a sideshow attraction. Yet when Gale's shelled star failed to materialize, all sideshow plans were indefinitely put on hold. What mattered most was salvaging his reputation, and as the whispers around town intensified, Gale recommitted himself to his cause.

Despite his efforts, throughout the spring, summer, and fall of 1949, Gale Harris's turtle-hunting attempts went continually unrewarded. While residents such as local garage worker Kenny Leitch were equally committed to Oscar's capture—concocting a multitude of tools and traps for that purpose—neither Kenny nor any other local turtle tinkerer ever managed to develop a weapon worthy of their adversary.

Gale Harris's team came closest to capturing Oscar on the evening of March 14, 1949, when several men took to the lake armed with floodlights and what they called a "young silo" trap—a drop cover constructed mostly of pipes and wheels. At one point, they allegedly had Oscar trapped (or *almost* trapped), though given his incredible size and strength, the men struggled to pull that stubborn beast back to shore. As the tug-of-war reached its climax, Oscar broke free, sending the turtle back to his murky home and Gale and Kenny back to their drawing board.

Days later, the turtle hunters took their search beneath the waterline, calling upon a pair of divers who took turns entering Fulk Lake's icy waters. On March 19, Woodrow Rigsby of Fort Wayne suited up in a deep-sea diving suit, though after several attempts, the helmet's sieve-like tendencies prevented him from continuing the search. A reel of silent film footage captured Rigsby's attempt, depicting a hundred or so shivering onlookers gathered along the shore while Gale Harris and an unidentified man fit the metal helmet over Rigsby's wool-hatted head. Camera flashes erupted throughout the silent footage, more closely resembling a red carpet than a turtle hunt—except, of course, for the backdrop. After the leaky helmet incident, a second diver, Walter Johnson, managed slightly better, spending a few hours beneath the water before finding himself chest-deep in mud and in need of assistance.

Spring slipped into summer, and while the crowd diminished, Gale

Harris, Kenny Leitch, and the newly recruited Walter Johnson continued their search for the turtle. Kenny Leitch and Walter Johnson spent much of the summer along the shoreline, their hopes buoyed upon learning that turtles rise to the surface at least two times daily—a fact they hoped to capitalize on. Meanwhile, Gale Harris kept his eye to his periscope, plumbing the depths via visual reconnaissance, while the others kept watch on the surface.

Of the turtle hunters' many creative trapping techniques, the most creative of all involved a two-hundred-pound female sea turtle, who they released into Fulk Lake in an effort to entice Oscar out of hiding. This, too, proved a failure, perhaps due to Oscar's monogamy; locals claimed he already had a girlfriend, whom they'd dubbed Myrtle.

None of it worked—not the nets, not the traps, not the divers, not even the girl.

Running low on options, Gale attempted a Hail Mary, one last crack at repairing his reputation.

"I'm gonna get that doggone turtle out of here if I have to drain the lake," Gale told the press. "I've been called a liar long enough."

True to his word, in late September and October of 1949, Gale invested a tractor, a piping system, and two thousand gallons of gasoline to the task of pumping out seventy million gallons of water, reducing the seven-acre lake to a single acre of sludge.

Despite the herculean dredging effort, no monstrous turtle emerged.

What Gale Harris did manage to dredge up was a megalomaniacal nature he didn't know he possessed, shades of Captain Ahab emerging within the mild-mannered farmer. It's a comparison that's been made before, notably by Gutowski, who added that it was "not difficult for an American mind to see something of the indomitable heathen prince of the seas" in their very own "small town Christian farmer."

By late November Gale was at last ready to give up the fight. He knew when he'd been beat, and after a bout of life-threatening appendicitis, he called off the search once and for all.

"When I laid up there on the verge of death," Gale said, "that's when I made up my mind that this thing was gonna stop."

Gale took his failing health as a sign from God, and in an effort not to be misunderstood, God offered a second sign, too.

On December 1, when Gale returned to his lake, he noticed that the rains had refilled it to its previous levels. All that time wasted, not to mention all those gallons of gas. The message couldn't have been clearer: if Oscar wanted to remain hidden, then nature would ensure that he was.

*

Sometimes we find the monster, sometimes the monster finds us. Though in the case of Gale Harris, not only did the monster find him, but it left its indelible mark.

I call it monster martyrdom: the phenomenon in which one's willingness to believe in the existence of a so-called monster undermines the believer's credibility in the eyes of the wider world. The phenomenon applies to various other hard-to-fathom subjects as well: from Bigfoot to UFOS. Linda Godfrey's work on the Beast of Bray Road is another example, though as she noted, her nonscientific career path ensured that she has no "scientific reputation to wreck."

All of which raises the question: Why is it so frowned upon to take incredible claims seriously?

Perhaps because in doing so, we disrupt our traditional understanding of our world. And what could be scarier than that?

For some, conceding that the natural world still maintains a few mysteries feels like admitting that science has failed. But science has not failed. Quite to the contrary, it regularly embraces the uncertainty while steering us toward something a little more certain. And I'm not just talking turtles here.

In December of 1938, after receiving a call from a sea captain about a strange fish discovered off the South African shore, thirty-two-year-old Marjorie Courtenay-Latimer, a curator for a local museum, headed over to the dock to see the oddity for herself.

"I picked away at the layer of slime to reveal the most beautiful fish I had ever seen," she said. Indeed, it was beautiful: five feet of "pale

Fig. 5. Fulk Lake in 2016. Courtesy of the author.

mauvy blue with faint flecks of whitish spots," all of which surely radi-
ated against the "iridescent silver-blue-green sheen."

Courtenay-Latimer carted her haul home in a taxi, and in the midst
of scouring every resource at her disposal, eventually consulted with
the museum's board chairman who hastily—and incorrectly—deemed
the specimen a rock cod.

Thankfully, Courtenay-Latimer knew better than to settle for the
easy answer, opting instead for the right one. Though she risked her
reputation in doing so, she bypassed the board president and asked for
a second opinion, handing over a sketch of the "rock cod" to a chem-
istry professor named J. L. B. Smith. Upon examining the sketch, a
dumbfounded Smith replied, "Lass, this discovery will be on the lips
of every scientist in the world."

He was right.

She'd recovered a coelacanth—a species of ancient fish thought
to have been extinct for over sixty-six million years. Often considered one of the greatest discoveries of the twentieth century, the

coelacanth astonished the world, not only for its ability to remain undetected throughout the eras, but also for what it might teach us as a "living fossil."

I shudder to imagine what might have been lost had Courtenay-Latimer decided not to go to the dock that day. Or what we might never have known had she agreed with the board president and classified the fish within the well-established taxonomy. After all, doing so would have been far easier than having to make a case for the incredible.

Yet she made her case nonetheless, stunning the world with her discovery and avoiding monster martyrdom all at once.

Courtenay-Latimer succeeded where Gale Harris failed, and for one reason: she had a specimen, whereas all Gale had was a story.

*

In the summer of 1971, twenty-eight-year-old John Gutowski, a doctoral student from Indiana University, drove to Churubusco in search of a story. He'd been teaching a folklore class at the burgeoning Fort Wayne branch of Indiana University, and while doing so, had learned from a student of the town's giant turtle.

"It intrigued the hell out of me," Gutowski tells me in a recent phone interview. "And once I went down there and realized it was a legend, it was a myth, it was all kinds of things, I realized it was going to be my dissertation topic."

Gutowski dedicated the summer of 1971 to Churubusco's most famous resident, and in the process, met many others as well. He rented a room in the town's center—directly above the local furniture store—and spent his days hauling his recording equipment from one household to the next, taking part in an ethnographic study that soon extended well beyond Oscar. For a folklorist like Gutowski, it was never a question of whether or not Oscar "existed"; what mattered most were the stories surrounding the creature.

"Whether it happened or not, whether it's true or not, whether there was a turtle or not, it was totally irrelevant," Gutowski explains. "It was a cultural phenomenon."

One perpetuated by the local citizenry's rich oral tradition. Everyone in town had a story to share, and Gutowski recorded many of them. Though one of the best stories, he tells me, managed to evade capture.

Sometime around midnight on Friday, July 27, 1971, as Gutowski prepared to return to his room after an evening of interviewing, he was approached on the street by an "impressive, articulate, authoritarian solemn figure" whom, for reasons of anonymity, Gutowski refers to as the "Philosopher."

"Are you the gentleman who's doing research on our turtle?" the Philosopher asked.

Gutowski confirmed that he was.

"Have you found much?"

Gutowski confirmed that he had.

"Well," the Philosopher said, "I think I may have something that you may not have found in your research."

Riveted, the young folklorist listened as the Philosopher began recounting some of the better known stories. But in the midst of the rehash he offered new information, too, particularly related to one capture attempt that allegedly took down a team of mules in the process.

"When they started pulling this turtle out, this turtle started burrowing down in this mud and he used nature's forces of that suction and he kept burrowing and those mules kept pulling, and, John, he ended up pulling that team of mules into that lake," the Philosopher said.

Then, with perfect comedic timing, the man paused, preparing for his punchline:

"It ended up that was the first piece of ass that turtle had in over one hundred years!"

Gutowski chuckles as he recounts the tale to me forty-six years later.

"He was so earnest and included so much factual material, and then the punchline comes, and you realize, 'Oh my God, I've been had.'"

In his dissertation, Gutowski offered a more scholarly response to his ribbing.

"Never in my short career as a folklorist have I been so devastatingly victimized by a tall tale," he wrote. "I had just completed participation in a classic folklore event: the greenhorn city boy done in by the cunning countryman."

Though Gutowski's midnight conversation with the Philosopher remains one of the most memorable moments of his research, perhaps his interviews with Gale Harris proved most valuable. Ironically, Gutowski's interviews with Gale weren't conducted in Churubusco, but in the hallways of the Fort Wayne branch of Indiana University, where Gutowski taught and Gale served as a janitor. Unbeknownst to Gutowski, they'd been sharing the hallways for months.

Upon learning of their fortuitous proximity, Gutowski began interviewing Gale in the evenings while the retired turtle hunter mopped the floors and collected the garbage.

"What were your impressions of Gale?" I ask.

"He was a very sincere man," Gutowski says. "And even twenty years after all the events, he was still insisting on what he saw."

*

In 1949 the *Churubusco Truth* named Gale Harris its Man of the Year, noting that "no man in the past one hundred years has done more to focus the attention of the nation on Churubusco."

For Gale, it was a dubious honor. Indeed, Churubusco had made a name for itself, but at the expense of Gale Harris's own good name.

"When people would talk about their recollections of what happened," Gutowski explains, "they'd very often end their narrative with something like, 'Oh, that turtle was a wonderful thing for Churubusco, but it sure ruined old Gale Harris.'"

Keep in mind that Gale Harris asked for none of this. Indeed, he made his turtle sighting public, and perhaps perpetuated the story by way of his efforts to catch it, though everyone I've talked to—and everything I've read—confirms that Gale was sincere in his desire to raise that monster from the muck. For him, it was always a hunt rather than a stunt; one he carried out to right the wrongs wrought against him.

Can we fault a man for attempting to dredge up the unimaginable? For taking a chance on a creature much as Marjorie Courtenay-Latimer had, though with a very different result? That Gale remained unwavering in his story is hardly surprising. We often remain committed to what we believe, even when evidence points us to the contrary. And let's give Gale some credit. After all, he was hardly alone in seeing Oscar. Plenty of other witnesses claimed to have seen him, too. Or to have seen a turtle, at least. Which, admittedly, is hardly front page news given that turtles are generally found in lakes. But Oscar was no ordinary turtle, mind you.

Oscar was extraordinary.

What if Gale Harris simply wanted to be extraordinary, too?

*

Upon entering Churubusco's Sheets and Childs Funeral Home, I'm greeted by thirty-two-year-old funeral home employee Miles Wilson. It's our first in-person meeting, though Miles and I had spoken by phone a few months prior when, out of the blue, I'd asked him if he wouldn't mind searching for a three-hundred-foot net in the basement of the funeral home.

"I know it's asking a lot," I'd conceded.

He'd indulged me, surprising us both by actually finding the net tucked inside a horse trough, just as Chuck Mathieu had said. The net's discovery served as a good excuse to return to Churubusco, offering me one last crack at getting to the bottom of the town's turtle story.

"Thanks for meeting me," I say, shaking Miles's hand inside the funeral home foyer. "I imagine you don't get a lot of calls about turtle nets."

"Well, we don't," Miles agrees, "but it's my pleasure."

He leads me down a stairwell to the concrete-floored basement—a wide room filled with a variety of the town's flotsam and jetsam.

"How'd the net find its way down here?" I ask.

"Well, people knew we had the room," Miles says, pushing past a few boxes until we come to the horse trough, "so I imagine someone just asked."

Over time, everyone seems to have forgotten who did the asking, who did the transporting, and who did the storing. But thank goodness someone did. In doing so, that someone preserved a bit of local history that would've been lost without the effort. Not only that, but a bit of *important* local history: one of the few items that ensures that Oscar is more than a myth.

Together, Miles and I reach into the trough and remove the net, a tangle of meshed material which we unroll a bit at a time. Gripping the webbing in my hands, I'm taken back to March 1949, when Gale Harris and his compatriots first unfurled it, stretching it across Fulk Lake in an effort to catch their creature.

Though he grew up in a nearby town, Miles and his family have many longstanding ties to Churubusco, as well as to the turtle story. Not only is Miles the great-grandson of Charlie Wilson, one of the two men who first spotted Oscar while fishing in July of 1948, but he's loosely related to Gale Harris, too. Though Miles's father was hesitant to return too often to the town ("Churubusco hasn't been the best for our family," he claimed), Miles—an upstanding Churubusco citizen and Rotary president—wears his turtle-related heritage with pride.

"I go to the McDonald's and see turtle pictures everywhere and am like, 'We're celebrities here.'"

If not them, certainly their turtle.

"So . . . is it all true?" I ask. "Did your great-grandfather Charlie and Ora Blue see a giant turtle while fishing that July afternoon in 1948?"

"I never met Charlie," Miles begins, "but my grandfather, when I'd talked to him about it, he'd chuckle and say, 'I'll tell you this, if you got those three together, Ora and Charlie could get Gale to believe anything.' But," Miles continues, "my grandfather was an honest man, and he would never have let Gale do all that if they hadn't seen something."

"So what do you think happened?"

"Well, Grandpa's theory always was . . ." He pauses as he considers how best to tell it. "Have you ever gone fishing?" he asks.

I nod.

"Did you catch a fish?"

I nod again.

"Now, when you told someone about that fish, how big was it?"

"The first time it was this big," I say, stretching my hands about a foot apart. "But the second time it was probably this big," I grin, stretching them wider.

"Not only that," Miles continues, "but if you tell someone about that trophy fish, and then that person goes and tells the next person, how big does that fish get?"

"Twice as big."

Miles nods.

"So, it's possible," he concludes, "that they saw a giant turtle. And it's possible, too, that the turtle they saw—when the story went on to the next person—it grew into this and that."

Any kindergartner who's ever played a game of telephone understands how quickly a story can spin out of control. How easy it is to lose the signal, relay a version of truth one version removed from the truth. To err is human, but to exaggerate is human, too. And as Miles knows all too well, an exaggerated turtle account might be the closest we ever come to the truth.

"Has Oscar helped Churubusco?" I ask. "Is there some benefit to having a giant turtle around town?"

"Oscar gave us a dot on the map," Miles says proudly. "Before him, Churubusco was not known."

*

Every town has its story, and every story needs its characters. While the cast of the Oscar saga stretches far and wide, Gale Harris always remains at its center: the "sober, upstanding farmer" who became his own worst enemy. In some ways, I can't help but think that Gale Harris became Oscar's stand-in: the spectacle that people could see.

Yet Gale Harris's legacy is more complicated than that. Of the many photographs of Gale I've seen, the most revealing depicts a middle-aged Gale standing along the shoreline. To his right are the two most dedicated members of his turtle-hunting team: Walter Johnson and Kenny Leitch. The trio appear proud of their efforts, a bib-overalled Gale offering the camera a toothy grin as he holds a spotlight between his hands. In the backdrop, we see the lake, and in the water, a slight ripple maneuvering around what appears to be a stick. What it does not appear to be is a turtle.

The picture's striking because it hints toward a truth not found anywhere in the news reports: these men were enjoying themselves. Despite the hardships to come, there was at least a brief time in the spring and summer of 1949 when Churubuscoans were having a little fun. In another photo, Gale Harris and his men can be seen posing alongside their turtle trap. And in another, they're holding tight to the tail of a sixty-five-pound snapper. Then there's the one where three men can be seen unravelling the three-hundred-foot net.

Much as Miles and I had, when we, too, were searching for proof of the impossible.

*

As my time in Churubusco winds down, I return to the history center to ask the Chucks the same question I've been asking everyone: Is Oscar real?

No matter who I ask, the answer only comes after a bit of hemming and hawing and a long, thoughtful stare into the distance. Some say yes, some say no, some say Oscar makes for a wonderful story.

The one fact everyone agrees on is Oscar's enormously positive impact on the town.

In addition to helping Churubusco earn its dot on the map, the town's Turtle Days festival brings in thousands of dollars annually. Without Oscar, there would be no Churubusco Park—the town's vast complex of baseball fields, batting cages, tennis courts, and a skate park, all of which were built from festival proceeds. Moreover, Oscar serves as the town's rallying point—part mascot, part myth, part curiosity.

As to the question of whether a four-hundred-pound turtle ever lurked in Fulk Lake, well, the Chucks are a little less sure.

Like most folks in town, they agree that "something" was seen, even if they can't confirm the size (or species) of the "something" in question.

"Does it ever feel disappointing," I ask them, "to have your most famous resident just . . . disappear?"

"Oh, I don't know," Chuck Jones shrugs. "I guess we're kind of glad he wasn't found. After all, the story's much better than the real thing."

Maybe he's right. As a result of his "bashfulness," Oscar gave Churubusco something much larger than a giant turtle. It gave the town its monster, its meaning, and a reason for tourists to pull to the side of the road.

Later that afternoon, I'll drive out to Fulk Lake and pull to the side of the road myself. Lifting my binoculars to my eyes, I'll peer out over the muck-covered water. I'll scan the area, searching every square inch for a ripple, or a displacement, or a dead-eyed turtle staring back.

Where is the sharp beak? The bone-plated shell bigger than a dining-room table?

All afternoon, all I'll see is nothing.

Except for a story just one glimpse away from burbling back to the surface.

Mothman

November 15, 1966–Present

NAME: MOTHMAN

SCIENTIFIC NAME: DEFIES CLASSIFICATION

LOCATION: POINT PLEASANT, WEST VIRGINIA, THOUGH SIGHTINGS OF
FLYING HUMANOIDS HAVE BEEN SPOTTED WORLDWIDE.

DESCRIPTION: A RED-EYED, GRAY-BODIED FLYING HUMANOID APPROXI-
MATELY SEVEN FEET TALL WITH A TEN-FOOT WINGSPAN.

FIELD NOTES: IN NOVEMBER OF 1966, TWO YOUNG MARRIED COUPLES
DROVE TO POINT PLEASANT, WEST VIRGINIA, WHERE THEY SPOTTED
WHAT WAS BELIEVED TO BE A FLYING HUMANOID NEAR THE CITY'S
MUNITIONS PLANT. SIMILAR SIGHTINGS PERSISTED FOR MONTHS.
MANY BELIEVE THE CREATURE TO HAVE PROPHETIC POWERS.

WITNESS TESTIMONY: "IT WAS LIKE A MAN WITH WINGS. IT WASN'T
LIKE ANYTHING YOU'D SEE ON TV OR IN A MONSTER MOVIE." STEVE
MALLETTE, NOVEMBER 16, 1966

CONCLUSION: UNSOLVED

Shortly before midnight on November 15, 1966, two young married couples—Roger and Linda Scarberry and Steve and Mary Mallette—drove from their homes in Point Pleasant, West Virginia, to an abandoned munitions plant just a few miles north of town. The munitions plant, known also as the "TNT area," had become a popular destination for joyriders, the remains of its eerie infrastructure well worth the eight-mile drive. Since the couples had a tank of gas and time to kill, they decided to pay it a visit.

Fig. 6. A statue of Mothman prominently displayed in Point Pleasant, West Virginia. EDLO Images©.

Eighteen-year-old Roger guided his black 1957 Chevy down the dirt road toward the munitions plant gate, slowly approaching the remnants of the North Power Plant. Though the munitions plant closed in 1945, ceding much of its property to the Department of Natural Resources, evidence of the land's previous life was everywhere. In its three years of operation, the West Virginia Ordnance Works had become a city unto itself, employing thirty-five hundred workers who busily produced a combined five hundred thousand pounds of TNT daily. It was an astonishing—some would say terrifying—amount. Yet following the events of November 15, it was only the second scariest thing to have occurred there.

As the couples pulled the car closer to the plant, they noticed something strange directly ahead of them—a pair of glowing red eyes refracting off the car's headlights. As their own eyes adjusted to the dark, the red eyes expanded to reveal a horrifying form: a grayish, humanoid creature. At seven feet tall, and with ten-foot wings stretched across its back, the creature resembled a human but was not one. It was barely more than a shadow, though a shadow that would stay with the young couples for the rest of their lives.

The riders had seen enough. As the creature effortlessly hurtled into the air with a flap of its wings, Roger spun the car around and sped off toward Route 62, the speedometer needle teetering perilously close to one hundred miles per hour. The creature kept pace, gliding above the car for several miles, at one point hovering a mere one hundred feet above them. At last they shook it—or thought they had—though as Roger directed the car back toward Point Pleasant's downtown, they spotted the creature again.

"It seemed to be waiting on us," Steve Mallette later remarked.

Yet this time, the car's headlights appeared to have startled the creature back into hiding, providing the riders safe passage to the Point Pleasant Sheriff's Office. Bursting through the front doors, they reported what they'd seen. Though their story was extraordinary, the sheriff's deputies and local police took their claims seriously; these were young people who could be trusted. At around 2:00 a.m., officers were dispatched to investigate the TNT site, keeping their eyes to the skies in search of anything resembling a red-eyed, winged creature. Flashlights cut through the dark, shining along the empty power plant, the boilers, the dusty road.

After a thorough search, the officers determined that whatever the couples had seen was no longer there.

Nonetheless, the Scarberrys and Mallettes stuck to their story.

"I'm a hard guy to scare," Roger Scarberry told reporters the morning after, "but last night I was for getting out of there."

*

In the immediate aftermath, residents of Point Pleasant struggled to come to grips with the sighting. No one quite knew what to make of the thing described as a "man-sized, bird-like creature."

One article described the creature as an enormous bird "with wings like an angel and legs like a man, seven feet tall with two large, red eyes about six inches apart."

It continued: "Officials at the [McClintic] Wildlife Station said no such description can be found in any of their fowl manuals."

"It was like a man with wings," Steve Mallette told the *Point Pleasant Register* on November 16. "It wasn't like anything you'd see on TV or in a monster movie."

Though, in fact, the Scarberrys and Mallettes' sighting had all the makings of a monster movie: the defunct military plant backdrop, the young coeds in the car, even a tire-screeching escape. In fact, thirty-six years later, the sighting served as fodder for a scene that actually made the big screen in the film version of *The Mothman Prophecies*, a Hollywood blockbuster that popularized the Mothman myth for a new generation.

I was a part of that generation. Though I'd never heard of any Mothman, the movie preview had piqued my interest enough to persuade me to fork over my six dollars. And so, one cold Friday evening in January of 2002, seventeen-year-old me and my thirteen-year-old brother took to the movie theater near our home.

Fig. 7. "Mothman" greets his fans outside the Mothman Museum in Point Pleasant, West Virginia. EDLO Images©.

Two hours later we left trembling, and we couldn't blame it on the winter's chill. Maybe it was Richard Gere's haunting portrayal of a grief-stricken reporter, whose inadvertent arrival in Point Pleasant fundamentally changed his life. Or maybe it came by way of Laura Linney's role as the baffled-but-believing local police officer. More than likely, however, our fear was the direct result of the film's depiction of the sketches of the red-eyed, winged creature which the witnesses claimed to have seen. The movie didn't need to *show* us Mothman, it merely needed to plant the seeds and allow them to take root in our imaginations.

And take root they did.

"But . . . it's just a movie, right?" my brother asked as we peered at the movie poster plastered outside the theater.

"Right," I said, leading us back toward the car. I didn't draw attention to the claim just a little lower on that poster: "Based on True Events."

As a result of the film's popularity, the Mothman story took on new life. In an effort to capitalize on the publicity, in 2005 Point Pleasant native Jeff Wamsley opened the Mothman Museum along the city's main drag. Marketed as the "The World's Only Mothman Museum" (no one disputes this), the downtown shop features an array of exhibitions consisting of newspaper reports, a life-sized replica of Mothman, and a collection of props used in the 2002 film.

As Jeff Wamsley tells me in a recent interview, Mothman serves as a perfect entry point to educate people on Point Pleasant's rich history. Much like Churubusco's Oscar the Turtle, Mothman helped the town earn a dot on the map. Not to mention a reason to pull to the side of the road. For the past sixteen years, people have not only pulled to the side of the road, but made a weekend of it, taking part in the annual Mothman Festival which occurs each fall, and which Jeff helps organize. Though he can't speak specifically to Mothman's economic impact on the town, Jeff tells me that most local businesses' biggest day of the year coincides with the festival.

While Mothman has done his part to spur the local economy, not every local is willing to buy his story. "I would say it's a split, with about 85 percent of the locals who think these people saw something and 15 percent who think the story was just fabricated to get some attention," Jeff says.

But for Jeff there's no question that the many witnesses saw something.

"They were not making up a story for attention," he says. "Many still refuse to talk about it." While Jeff concedes that Mothman left no physical proof behind, for him, the accumulated witness testimony serves as all the proof he needs to believe that *something* was seen during a thirteen-month stretch between 1966 and 1967—and long after as well.

Despite decades of theorizing by those both in and beyond Point Pleasant, Jeff doesn't believe we'll ever know for certain just what those witnesses saw.

What can be explained—and, in fact, was in a 1966 *Herald-Dispatch* article by Ralph Turner—has to do with the long-term effects of the sightings.

"Just what was seen in the dark of the night may never be firmly established," Turner confirmed. But maybe, the journalist mused, "a new tourist attraction has been born."

Thanks to Jeff Wamsley, a new tourist attraction was born—thirty-nine years later.

*

Today, if you venture deep enough into the McClintic Wildlife Management Area—the former "TNT area" where the Scarberry and Mallette sighting occurred—you're guaranteed a glimpse of West Virginia's most famous monster. Or at least a spray-painted version, whose image has taken up residence on an interior wall inside one of the many subterranean TNT Storage Igloos that remain. There are his unmistakable red eyes and greenish wings, a larger than life reminder of the rash of Mothman sightings that still loom large in the local citizenry's memories several decades before.

In its current version, the Mothman's spray-painted depiction also includes various sexual appendages tagged atop the creature's body, throwing the creature's gender into serious question. I like to think the graffiti artist's "additions" offer insight on the current state of the Mothman myth—a sign that the creature is no longer something to be feared, but a story to be spun, altered, even mocked. Just a bit of local lore that took on new life rather than being forgotten.

Because Mothman is not forgotten. In fact, some argue that flying humanoids of Mothman's ilk are making a resurgence.

Not in Point Pleasant, West Virginia, but—of all places—Chicago, Illinois.

Between April and July 2017, over twenty flying humanoid sightings were reported throughout Chicago. Beginning on April 7, when a woman walking her dog spotted a seven-foot-tall creature with folded wings standing in Oz Park on the city's north side.

"I felt like this thing could see right through me, read me, it knew what I was thinking, like it could stare right into my very soul," the witness reported. "It was the most terrified I have ever been in my life."

Soon there were other sightings. In April of 2017, while walking along

Damen Street at 2:00 a.m., one witness spotted "the biggest freaking owl I have ever seen." Less than two weeks later, a father and son walking near the Calumet River observed something "unlike any bird we have seen in our lives." In June of 2017, a couple taking a nighttime stroll through Lincoln Park had their own encounter. "I thought it was an eagle or a bat," the witness reported, "but it was definitely bigger than both of those." As the sightings continued, Lon Strickler—researcher, author, and blogger of all things paranormal—took note. In fact, he'd been taking note since the Chicago sightings first began, gathering various accounts and diligently sharing them on his website, Phantoms & Monsters.

By late July, when the *Chicago Tribune* saw fit to run a story on the phenomenon, the creature had acquired several names, including the Chicago Phantom and the Chicago Owlman. But despite its various names, no one could say precisely what it was. A wayward bird? A giant bat? A hoax?

"I have long theorized that the Mothman, and other unknown winged beings, are multidimensional lifeforms . . . that can be summoned by high-energy incorporeal entities that reside on our Earth plane," Lon Strickler told the *Chicago Tribune*.

A multidimensional what? A high-energy who? Admittedly, it was not an answer I'd expected to hear, nor one I much understood.

When I call Lon for clarification, he tries explaining it to me, though admits, too, that "at this point right now, I really have no idea what it is."

Which puts him in good company with the rest of the world.

"We're working on a few things," Lon explains, "but there's nothing solid enough that I want to comment on." While he believes the multidimensional theory remains the most promising lead, he concedes, too, that "we really don't understand it ourselves."

Despite all that we don't know, Lon believes we're inching ever closer to finding answers, adding that he thinks science is "on the cusp of proving that there's a certain number of these alternative universes or alternative realities."

Ask any cosmologist, physicist, or sci-fi buff, and they'll all tell you there's no shortage of conversation pertaining to multiverses, or parallel universes, or alternative universes. No shortage, either, of conversations surrounding so-called windows and doorways that might lead us between one multiverse or another. Or in the case of Mothman, a window or doorway that might lead something else into *our* universe.

During our chat in Vasili's Corner Café, Linda Godfrey had made a similar suggestion related to the Beast of Bray Road's entrance into our world, referring to such creatures as "multitalented beings." According to Linda, and supported by Lon, creatures such as unknown upright canines and flying humanoids may possess the capability of traveling between worlds.

"It's like rather than reality being completely solid or completely etheric and ghostlike, there's more of a sliding scale of reality," Linda had told me. "Which I think ties in pretty well with most things in the universe. Very few things are completely black and white."

It's that mysterious middle ground that so often proves perplexing. For a nonscientist such as myself, all this talk of dimensions and multiverses seems much too theoretical. I'm more comfortable dealing with tangible proof—preferably a specimen or some trace of one (hair, a footprint, a bone). Is it asking too much for Mothman to be a giant bat, and Oscar to be an exaggerated turtle, and the Beast of Bray Road to be gray wolf with a spring in his step?

In all of these cases, I've been looking for a flesh and blood answer, though as Linda and Lon indicate, it's not always that simple. After all, we're dealing with the unknown. And the unknown is where these creatures thrive.

*

In the early evening of July 24, 2017, Lon Strickler's telephone rang. On the other end was a distraught man who claimed to have seen a human-like creature leap from Willis Tower less than an hour and a half before.

"The witness states that the being's outstretched wings were not very large, maybe 6–8 [feet] from tip to tip, but were very jagged and insect-like (shaped similar to a moth)," Lon reported. "The being was also dark green in color and had a body form like that of a mantis."

The witness's description deviated greatly from the previous sightings. This was no bat-like creature as others had claimed to have seen, but something that seemed to fit more neatly within the insect world. The giant, human-like insect world, that is. Yet since Lon's description referenced the word "moth," I'm immediately pulled back to Point Pleasant.

Did West Virginia's monster simply fly west?

"I think it's the same *type* of being," Lon tells me, though he doubts it's the same exact being.

While Lon finds the Willis Tower sighting compelling, he's hesitant to accept the witness's testimony at face value.

"It's hard to imagine how [the witness] got the description he did at such a distance. I mean, if that thing had come off [the building] at the height he said it did, then it's pretty hard to see much detail."

I agree.

"And how is it that no one else on a busy Chicago street managed to confirm the sighting?" I ask. "I mean, a human-sized insect would draw some attention, right?"

"That's another thing we don't understand," Lon says. "These things show up in huge crowds sometimes, but it seems only certain people see it. Either that or some people just aren't concerned about it. Or," he adds, "they're too ashamed or embarrassed to mention it."

*

Shame, embarrassment, and humiliation are but a few of the forms monster martyrdom tends to take. But when people do talk, there's always someone to listen, always some curiosity seeker willing to take down the "facts." People like Linda Godfrey, the Churubusco Chucks, and Lon Strickler, just to name a few.

But long before their entrance upon the scene, there were others. And amid the backdrop of the 1966–67 Mothman sightings, that curiosity seeker was named John A. Keel. Thirty-six-year-old Keel, a journalist and ufologist, was busily tracking ufo sightings throughout the

South when he read a newspaper article about Mothman sightings in Point Pleasant. He traveled there soon after, and over the next several years, gathered as much evidence as he could on the phenomena, the result of which became the basis for his 1975 cult classic, *The Mothman Prophecies*.

Even after a cursory reading, it's clear that Keel's book is a far cry from the movie version. While the 2002 film centers on Mothman itself, Keel's book filters the Mothman phenomenon through a much wider lens, linking Mothman sightings alongside a vast array of supernatural events alleged to have occurred throughout the region during that time.

Keel's book recounts what he calls a "tapestry of the paranormal," though in my estimation, it reads more like a smorgasbord. Within its pages, readers find a bit of everything: Mothman, sure, but also UFOs, strange tracks, garbled telephone calls, Men in Black, mutilated animals, portals, demons, and disappearing pets, just to name a few.

The story is difficult to believe, especially when one's searching for a singular trail worth following amid these widely scattered bread crumbs. Keel, aware of such criticism, assures readers in his book's opening pages that he has little interest in "the manifestations of the phenomenon." Instead, he claims to be pursuing "the source of the phenomenon itself."

"To do this," he continues, "I have objectively divorced myself from all the popular frames of reference."

You'll hear no quarrel from me. Though its entertainment value is beyond dispute, to read *The Mothman Prophecies* as a source of credible information is to undermine our more logical selves. Yet while reading it in the midst of writing my own book, I can't help but see a bit of Keel's own prophetic powers at work.

"Some future investigator of the paranormal may wander into these [West Virginian] hills someday, talk with these people, and write a whole chapter of a learned book on demonology repeating this piece of folklore," he writes. "Other scholars will pick up and repeat his story in their books and articles."

Am I the one writing the "learned book," the scholar repeating the story?

And in doing so, am I steering readers one version further removed from the truth? Adding to an echo chamber that's already deafening?

After all, what could I possibly know that past scholars didn't? What new clue—in a new context—might change everything?

*

Do you want to know what West Virginians were seeing for thirteen months in 1966–67?

I'll tell you.

They were seeing a giant bat, or a giant owl, or a giant weather balloon. Or a prophetic demon, or an angel of death, or something somewhere in between.

But maybe there's another worldly explanation, one that has less to do with multiverses than migration patterns.

Enter the sandhill crane—one of nature's loveliest (albeit gangliest) avian species.

Of the many Mothman possibilities, the sandhill crane theory is the one I like the most. Perhaps because I'm a birder, though perhaps, too, because of what I've learned while birding; namely, how easy it is to misidentify one species for another. Sometimes wildly so.

I'm hardly alone in propagating the sandhill crane theory. In fact, within days of the Scarberrys and Mallettes' November 1966 sighting, Dr. Robert Smith, associate professor of wildlife biology at West Virginia University, was already making a strong case for the crane.

"From all the descriptions I have read about this 'thing' it perfectly matches the sandhill cranes," Dr. Smith said simply. "I definitely believe that's what these people are seeing."

Keel disagreed. Though he noted the "rash of strange birds" whose sudden appearance in nearby Ohio and Pennsylvania fit within the timeline of Point Pleasant's Mothman sightings, he wasn't persuaded by the explanation. To test Dr. Smith's theory, Keel kept a picture of a sandhill crane in his briefcase at all times and regularly shared it with witnesses. At no point, according to Keel, did a Mothman witness claim that what he or she had seen in any way resembled that particular bird.

Yet we can't overlook the descriptions the witnesses provided themselves—a few of which synced neatly alongside descriptions of the crane. Some reported the creature appeared ostrich-like, was grayish in color, and stood approximately seven feet tall. Keel noted, too, that several witnesses reported a "reddish cast" around the creature's eyes.

Much of which confirmed Dr. Smith's theory.

Major discrepancies, however, have to do with the bird's size and speed. Whereas Mothman witnesses described a creature seven feet tall with a ten-foot wingspan and travelling upward of seventy miles per hour, the sandhill crane's dimensions, wingspan, and speed are all generally about half that.

And another problem: sandhill cranes don't typically travel that far east. What they might be doing east of the Ohio River is a mystery, though a wayward bird—or even a wayward flock—is hardly impossible to imagine. (And a lot more likely, it seems, than some of the alternatives.)

The most pertinent question, however, is whether any sandhill cranes were spotted in Point Pleasant, West Virginia, during the thirteen-month stretch when the majority of Mothman sightings occurred. Or for that matter, at any point in Point Pleasant's history.

I find the answer to the latter in a 1960 article titled "Migration of the Sandhill Crane East of the Mississippi River." In it, ornithologist and crane expert Lawrence Walkinshaw makes specific reference to a previous sighting of a sandhill crane in Point Pleasant in September of 1934. I'm astonished by the mention, and astonished, too, that as far as I know, no one has ever submitted this "evidence" into the Mothman record.

Not that a 1934 sandhill crane sighting necessarily serves as the explanation for the 1966–67 sightings, though it does add one new piece to the puzzle. A piece that surely supports Dr. Smith's assessment.

Other alleged sandhill crane sightings would, temporally speaking, soon hit even closer to home. In early December 1966—just weeks after the Scarberrys and Mallettes' sighting—five pilots were gathered on the Gallipolis airstrip just across the Ohio River from Point Pleasant. As they peered into the sky they spotted what at first they assumed was a plane. But they changed their minds upon watching the unidentified "thing" in the sky swoop sharply downward, soaring at speeds of around seventy miles per hour and dropping as low as three hundred feet from the ground.

"The most outstanding characteristic they noticed," one newspaper reported, "was the unusually long neck, which was estimated to be about 4 feet in length. The men substantiated evidence that it was a sandhill crane."

Substantiated, perhaps, though their sighting did not crack the case outright.

After all, a single sandhill crane sighting in Gallipolis, Ohio, doesn't necessarily explain Point Pleasant's many Mothman sightings.

What if there were two creatures soaring through the skies?

And what if the sandhill crane was simply the Mothman's red herring?

*

Whatever it was—or whatever it *is*—another question remains: What does its presence mean?

If the Mothman is a sandhill crane, then its presence is pretty simple: here's a bird that got a little off course.

But if the Mothman is some version of flying humanoid, then that question becomes far more complicated. Many have claimed the creature to be an "omen of doom." And in the case of the Point Pleasant sightings, that "doom" manifested itself on the evening of Friday, December 15, 1967, when shortly after 5:00 p.m., the Silver Bridge connecting Point Pleasant with Gallipolis, Ohio, suddenly collapsed, sending thirty-one vehicles into the frigid Ohio River. According to historian Chris LeRose, many locals were "out buying Christmas trees, enjoying the holiday season, unaware of the disaster, until they heard the sound."

What a terrible sound it was, one described by witnesses as a "shotgun blast" and a "sonic boom." It was a sound that soon became much more than a sound, a small crack in an eyebar sending the bridge tumbling into the river. Forty-six people were killed, marking the event with the dubious distinction of being one of the deadliest bridge collapses in U.S. history.

John Keel's *The Mothman Prophecies* set forth the theory of a connection between Mothman's appearance and the bridge collapse—a connection used to great cinematic effect in the 2002 film. But life extends beyond Hollywood, and some locals have taken offense to such tenuous and unprovable claims. Why focus on Mothman, the thinking goes, when we ought to focus on the real issue: structural deficiencies in our infrastructure?

Perhaps because Mothman's so-called prophetic potential makes for a great story. And one that fits neatly into the many other stories of flying humanoids said to have appeared prior to major disasters. Most notably the tale of the Blackbird of Chernobyl, which was alleged to have been seen soaring over the Ukrainian nuclear plant in the weeks leading up to the disaster. Or so claimed a character in the film version of *The Mothman Prophecies*.

Cryptozoologist Loren Coleman dismissed the claim, noting that there was "not one thread of evidence that any winged weirdies were witnessed before the Chernobyl accident. It is a bit of movie fiction that has, unfortunately, moved into pseudo-factoid cryptozoology."

Though flying humanoids' alleged prophetic powers don't begin and end with Mothman. Other alleged sightings have been linked to the 2007 Minnesota bridge collapse, a swine flu outbreak in Mexico, even 9/11. Then again, it's always easy to point fingers to "premonitions" in the aftermath. And easier still to see a causal connection when that connection helps spin a better yarn.

The irony is that while some have pegged Mothman as Point Pleasant's "omen of doom," the city's most direct link to death and destruction has nothing to do with the creature, but the locale where Mothman was first sighted by the Scarberrys and Mallettes. Need I remind you that in its heyday, the West Virginia Ordnance Works produced half a million pounds of TNT daily?

What's a better indicator of death and destruction than that?

*

Fig. 8. Acid Area Laboratory and Supervisor's Office, West Virginia Ordnance Works, near where the Scarberrys and Mallettes' Mothman sighting occurred on November 15, 1966. Courtesy of Wikimedia Commons.

In the days following the November 15, 1966, sighting, Point Pleasant's on-edge citizens did what we often do: grabbed guns, joined a posse, and prepared to get that creature in their crosshairs. For them, nothing could be more certain than a downed specimen.

Wildlife biologist and McClintic's manager Duane Pursley remarked that so many people had come to the refuge armed with guns that they'd considered closing the area to the public.

Others reported a more festive mood, including Roger Bennett of the *Athens Messenger*, who noted the hundreds of people crowding into the TNT area night after night.

"Every intersection was jammed with parked cars and small camps of laughing," Bennett wrote, describing, too, the "jostling young adults" as well as the "huge abandoned power plant buildings" that "rang with the shrieks of youngsters, scaring themselves."

By late November, authorities from the McClintic Wildlife Management Area remained certain that the large bird (assuming it was one) would soon be flushed by the more than two hundred deer hunters that entered the area daily. But somehow, amid all the attention the TNT area received, the creature remained out of sight. Or at least out of the crosshairs.

But that changed on the evening of December 20, 1966, when farmer Ace Henry of Gallipolis Ferry—a mere seven miles south of Point Pleasant—spotted a large winged creature roosting atop his barn. Believing it to be a hawk, he took to his twenty-gauge shotgun, aimed, and fired.

Upon inspecting the freshly downed creature, he was surprised to learn that he hadn't shot a hawk at all.

What he'd shot was Mothman. Or at least the creature that might've been mistaken for it.

Stretched before him on the ground was a snowy owl—a second rare bird for the region. With a five-foot wingspan and white feathers with black speckles, it was indeed a sight to behold. But probably not the Mothman.

Fast forward thirty-six years, however, and another owl enters into the Mothman mythos. In 2002, amid the hullabaloo surrounding the release of *The Mothman Prophecies*, Joe Nickell, senior research fellow for the Committee for Skeptical Inquiry, argued that Mothman was likely nothing more than a common barn owl. He argued that the owl not only fit the range, habitat, and general description, but due to its nocturnal nature, was unfamiliar to many locals as well.

As for Mothman's red eyes, Nickell relied upon the expertise of ornithologist Frank B. Gill, who noted that some birds' eyes appear red when a flashlight or headlights are shone their way. "This 'eyeshine' is not the iris color but that of the vascular membrane—the tapetum—showing through the translucent pigment layer on the surface of the retina."

I find myself nodding throughout much of Nickell's assessment, including his acknowledgement that there is "unlikely to be a single explanation."

It's possible, after all, that in some instances Mothman was a giant bat, or a giant owl, or a giant weather balloon, while in other instances it was a wayward crane or a barn owl. But as Nickell makes clear, what folks likely didn't see was a multidimensional being set foot upon our planet to offer portends of doom.

"We are thus faced with a choice between a plausible, naturalistic explanation on the one hand," Nickell wrote, "and a fanciful, incredible one on the other, the evidence for which is based solely on the most undependable evidence: reports by excited witnesses."

Sobering as it is, such a clear-eyed assessment offers the kind of logical conclusion I'm desperate to hear, a counterpoint to the stranger theories I've heard.

Which is not to discount those theories, but to shed light upon them. Light that, with any luck, refracts back with a better answer.

*

All of which leaves us where exactly?

Having to choose between Mothman being a sandhill crane or an owl? A weather balloon or a bat? Or is it what Lon Strickler believes it might be: a visitor from an unknown multiverse?

"What are we to do?" I ask Lon. "How do we come to any conclusions about any of this?"

"We keep our eyes open and we keep an open mind," Lon says simply.

I nod. It's something we can both agree on.

Maybe it's a bird, maybe it's a plane, maybe it's Mothman.

Keep your eyes to the skies. We may just find out together.

Part 2

MARTIANS

The supernatural is the natural not yet understood.

ELBERT HUBBARD

Joe Simonton's Space Pancakes

April 18, 1961

NAME: JOE SIMONTON'S SPACE PANCAKES

SCIENTIFIC NAME: N/A

LOCATION: EAGLE RIVER, WISCONSIN

DESCRIPTION: ON THE MORNING OF APRIL 18, 1961, JOE SIMONTON WAS ALLEGEDLY VISITED BY AN UNIDENTIFIED FLYING OBJECT THAT LANDED IN HIS BACKYARD. SIMONTON WAS GREETED BY THE THREE BEINGS WITHIN, WHO WERE SAID TO BE APPROXIMATELY FIVE FEET TALL, 125 POUNDS, AND RESEMBLED "ITALIANS." THEY REQUESTED WATER, HE PROVIDED IT, AND IN EXCHANGE, HE RECEIVED FOUR SO-CALLED SPACE PANCAKES.

WITNESS TESTIMONY: "I RAN OUTSIDE AND SAW A HATCHWAY OR DOOR-WAY OPEN AND A SMALL PERSON ABOUT FIVE FEET TALL APPEAR IN THE HATCHWAY, AND AS I APPROACHED, HE SIGNALED FOR WATER."

JOE SIMONTON, 1961

CONCLUSION: UNSOLVED

On April 18, 1961, sixty-year-old Joe Simonton—a plumber from Eagle River, Wisconsin—had just begun scrubbing the breakfast dishes when he spotted a flying saucer descending from the sky.

"There it was, coming straight down like an elevator," Joe later remarked. He rushed outside his rural cabin, tilted his head skyward, and spotted a chrome-colored craft—about thirty feet in diameter and twelve feet at the center—lowering itself toward the yard. As the craft

Fig. 9. Members of J. Allen Hynek's research team collect evidence on the Simonton property, Eagle River, Wisconsin, 1961. Courtesy of the Center for UFO Studies.

hovered just a few feet above the ground (it resembled "two large soup bowls put together" Joe claimed), a hatch sprung wide, revealing three short men inside. They resembled "Italians," Joe recalled (five feet tall and 125 pounds), each of them busying themselves at various tasks. One worked a control board, another manned a flameless griddle, while the third engaged with Joe directly, extending a water jug in need of filling.

Joe, being neighborly, was happy to oblige. He reached for the jug, filled it in his basement sink, then returned it to the parched space travelers. Upon doing so, Joe made himself at home, taking the liberty of placing his hand on the craft and peeking inside the hatch.

I can't help but envision this moment as the interstellar equivalent of the "Whatcha got under the hood?" conversation so often overheard at car shows. Yet for Joe, it didn't much matter what was "under the hood" but what was going on inside the craft itself. His cursory glance revealed a mostly black wrought iron interior interspersed with instrument panels. Listening closely, his ears picked up a sound akin to a generator hum.

If you remove the spaceship from the scene, this encounter doesn't seem all that out of the ordinary. After all, here were human-looking people doing human-like things. The interaction might've easily been mistaken for a backyard cookout or a neighborhood tailgate.

Though again, only if you remove the spaceship.

Joe, seemingly unmoved by the encounter, attempted to strike up a conversation with his Martian interlopers. Nodding toward the "Italian" working the griddle ("dressed in black, but with a narrow red trim along the trouser," newspapers reported), he pantomimed lifting a utensil to his lips.

"What I meant was 'are you eating,'" Joe later explained. As if to confirm it, the strange little man allegedly handed Joe four pancakes, each about three inches in diameter. A parting gift, perhaps, or a thank-you for Joe's hospitality.

Joe graciously accepted the gift, though before he could properly thank the men, the hatch clicked shut and the saucer burst back into the sky.

Perplexed, Joe craned his neck up toward the clouds, then down toward his pancakes.

And then, he lifted a cake to his lips and took a bite.

*

If there's a food less befitting than pancakes to commemorate a historic meeting between humans and extraterrestrials, I am unaware of it. To my mind, pancakes, the most pedestrian of breakfast food, sends a clear message to its eaters:

Sorry, we ran out of waffles.

Mightn't these travelers—who'd allegedly journeyed across the universe—have prepared something a little less passé? Was an eggs Benedict out of the question? And might I suggest a side of hollandaise sauce? Of course, for all I know, pancakes may be the pinnacle of extraterrestrial cuisine. And offering Joe four of them might've been meant to serve as a bit of pancake diplomacy, an edible olive branch to share between our species. One thing I know for certain: I'd take a pancake over a probe any day.

It's hard not to poke fun at the prospect of interplanetary pancakes. Hard, too, to reconcile Joe's apparent don't-think-twice approach to eating one. Though perhaps it was his way to show his appreciation, an action akin to heads of state exchanging cultural gifts in the interest of friendship. Though the problem with this theory is that Joe took his first bite *after* the saucer vanished.

Which points us toward a slightly less-compelling motive:

That Joe ate the space pancake because he was hungry. Or curious. Or both.

What we know is that Joe did not enjoy the experience. In fact, one reason he believed he'd been visited by space aliens—as opposed to say, actual Italian pilots out for a spin in the latest in aircraft technology— was due to the vast difference in palate.

"If they ate the pancakes like they gave me their taste sure was different from mine," Joe remarked. "To me these pancakes tasted like cardboard."

Let the record show that Joe Simonton was no food critic. In fact, Joe—who passed away in 1972—was no scientist, no UFOlogist, no expert on the mysteries of the world. Aside from conversations he may have shared with a local Vilas County judge named Frank Carter—a UFO enthusiast and member of the National Investigations Committee on Aerial Phenomena (NICAP)—it's possible he'd never even heard of a UFO.

Nevertheless, Joe wasn't afraid by what he'd seen.

"I try to live right and I don't think there is much to be afraid of," he later said. "These men were friendly to me and I was friendly to them."

Joe—the small town Wisconsin plumber—seemed an unlikely candidate to serve as ambassador for Earth. Though perhaps his "golden rule" mentality made him perfectly suited for the task. He had no preconceptions about the visitors (or their cuisine), and thus, treated them as he would his far more local neighbors.

If he had something to fear he didn't know it. And he wouldn't have, unless he'd gone to the movies.

*

The 1950s and early 1960s were a golden age for American sci-fi cinema. One could hardly sit down with a box of popcorn without a Martian or two overrunning planet Earth. From 1951's *The Day the Earth Stood Still* to 1963's *The Day Mars Invaded Earth*, the invasion seemed truly endless: one Hollywood production after another shaping America's consciousness. There was no escape. Except, of course, that these movies were our escape.

In her 1965 essay, "The Imagination of Disaster," critic Susan Sontag pondered the impact of science fiction films on society at-large, writing that 1960s Americans lived "under continual threat of two equally fearful, but seemingly opposed, destinies: unremitting banality and inconceivable terror." On one hand, we appeared to have slipped into the quiet comforts of conformity, while on the other, we remained under near-constant threat of nuclear annihilation by a country half the world away. Sci-fi films, Sontag argued, "serve[d] to allay" our anxieties. "They inculcate[d] a strange apathy concerning the processes of radiation, contamination, and destruction."

Following the catastrophic destruction at Hiroshima and Nagasaki, we'd indeed propelled ourselves headlong into the atomic age. Which Americans loved at first, right up until the Soviets perfected their own nuclear weapon in August of 1949. At which point our relationship with the bomb became more complicated. It's one thing to have one's finger on the button, but quite another to be in the crosshairs.

By comparison, flying saucers and melon-headed Martians served as a much-needed relief—a bit of fantasy indulged for the price of a movie ticket. Moreover, despite the brinksmanship often displayed in the alien vs. human sci-fi films of the era, Sontag argued that "the bellicosity of science fiction films is neatly channeled into the yearning for peace, or for at least peaceful coexistence."

Forget pancake diplomacy, this was silver screen diplomacy—and it appeared to be working.

In the midst of the Cold War, these films served a timely lesson: a reminder, at least allegorically, that despite our differences, it was better to be different than dead.

Yet Joe may have never considered such dire dilemmas. Instead, he wrestled with different questions: To fill or not to fill the water jug? To eat or not to eat the pancake? He'd opted to do both, of course, and as a result of his hospitality and adventurous appetite, he soon became the central character of a story ripe for the big screen.

Though Joe's story was destined to play out on a much smaller screen: in the form of a self-published pamphlet he penned in May of 1961. Which is not to imply that there wasn't great interest in Joe's tale; indeed, there was. For weeks the story ran wild, the local news reporting that residents were "surprised and almost bewildered by the tremendous interest in the report." And no one was more bewildered than Joe. No Hollywood directors came knocking, though for two months most everyone else did, resulting in a level of attention that soon proved overwhelming for the modest midwesterner who preferred to keep to himself. "No one knows just what I have been through these last two months," Joe remarked. "I lost the first three weeks work and two good plumbing jobs on account of this flying saucer."

He felt put out by the experience, and in some ways resented it. Not only had he lost some good plumbing work, but a few publications had mistakenly characterized him as a "chicken farmer"—an unforgivable trespass, and to Joe's mind, the part of the story that required the most immediate attention. Though the media offered a number of insinuations related to Joe's mental state, it was the chicken farmer line that appeared to give him the most grief. "I am a plumber and not a chicken farmer," he made clear early in his pamphlet. "I keep some chickens mostly for my own use. Some papers say I am a chicken farmer but I am not. I just want the people to know the truth about everything."

If anyone knew how to bury a lede, it was Joe Simonton. Certainly no one purchased a copy of *The Story of the Flying Saucer* to learn the full extent of Joe's chicken farming, though this hardly kept him from dedicating some prime real estate to the topic. For Joe, the details were important, and he stood his ground on all fronts.

Yes, he *had* seen Italian-looking men in a flying saucer.

And no, he wasn't a chicken farmer.

*

On the morning of April 26, 1961, UFO researcher and Northwestern University astrophysicist Dr. J. Allen Hynek received a phone call from the Duluth Air Defense Sector in Minnesota, informing him of Joe Simonton's encounter. Hynek, who in addition to his other duties, served as the scientific advisor for Project Blue Book—the air force's half-hearted effort to investigate UFO sightings—was dispatched to Eagle River to assess the validity of Joe Simonton's claims. Hynek, accompanied by a pair of graduate students, left immediately, arriving in the small north-central Wisconsin town later that afternoon.

After a bit of searching, Hynek and his team eventually found their way to Joe's property, a rustic cabin on an unkempt yard located a few miles outside of town. Joe's wife, Mary, had been working in a Chicago department store for two years, leaving her husband and his chickens mostly to themselves. That is, except for the visitors they'd allegedly received on the morning of April 18.

Hynek took careful note of Joe's secluded living situation, eventually echoing a sentiment offered by Vilas County judge and local UFO enthusiast Frank Carter, who'd remarked that it was possible Joe had simply become "shack happy" during his time alone.

Though the media was quick to characterize Joe Simonton as a country bumpkin, Hynek took the man seriously. At least as seriously as the situation allowed.

"In view of the fact that it is not our practice to investigate cases in which there is only one observer," Hynek remarked, "this case should not be given too much weight and certainly one cannot expect any sort of a definitive solution."

Joe's encounter required confirmation, and without it, investigators like Hynek were hesitant to involve themselves too deeply. Moreover, Hynek added, judging by "the appearance of the man, his habits of life and his evident loneliness, it would appear to me that the situation was ripe for suggestibility and a mental aberration."

Yet throughout Hynek's afternoon and evening questioning his subject, he concluded, too, that there was much to be admired in Joe's testimony, limited as it was. "[Joe] answered questions directly, did not contradict himself, insisted on the facts being exactly as he stated and he refused to accept embellishments or modifications."

According to many, Joe Simonton was a reliable source.

Making his story all the more difficult to discount.

*

Of the many "strange" stories I've explored, perhaps Joe Simonton's is the strangest. Amid all the talk of pancakes and "Italians" and rural Wisconsin–bound spacecrafts, it's easy to lose one's sense of fact and fiction. I know when I'm licked, so I call up writer and anomalist Jerome Clark for a bit of much-needed clarity. Author of *Unexplained! Strange Sightings, Incredible Occurrences, and Puzzling Physical Phenomena*, among many others, Jerry has dedicated over half a century to exploring the world's anomalies. From fairies to lake monsters to strange shapes in the sky, he's left his mark on an array of strange subjects, curating one doorstopper-sized compendium after another overflowing with his extensive scholarship. He's no stranger to Joe Simonton's space pancakes, and when I ask what makes Joe's story unique, he surprises me by telling me it's not. At least not entirely.

"I suppose in some ways it's unique, but in other ways it's kind of characteristic of high strangeness experiences," Jerry explains. "You're not going to prove anything from the incident, but on the other hand, it's pretty hard to explain conventionally unless Joe Simonton was crazy or dishonest, and as far as I know there's no evidence of that."

Jerry tells me that when examining a strange event such as this, investigators are often dependent on witness testimony. And he understands—just as Dr. Hynek did—the limitations of a single firsthand account. Nevertheless, he believes that most people who report strange phenomena truly believe what they've seen. Which does not mean that what witnesses claim to see is necessarily what it is; but rather, that there is rarely a nefarious plot in the report itself.

"Even the air force, whose investigation of UFOS was conducted with nothing but ill will, acknowledged that hoaxes are fairly rare," Jerry says. "They're not nonexistent, of course, but most hoaxes that Blue Book found were photographs of contrived evidence. And yes there are people who lie, and you always have to be alert to that possibility. But overwhelmingly," he continues, "people tell these stories sincerely and often reluctantly."

As an example, he tells me just how often people report seeing fairies, though they mostly refrain from using the word, which connotes magic, myth, and, of course, fairy tales. "They have an experience that they don't dare tell anybody about, but what they describe is the classic experience of fairy folk. These things are really ubiquitous," he adds. "What isn't ubiquitous is people's willingness to talk about them."

Jerry confirms what Linda Godfrey had told me previously: that there's a social cost involved.

"Ridicule really enforces silence," he says. "Ridicule keeps the boundaries firm. And people don't want to be ridiculed, of course."

"Have you paid a price as a result of your research interests?" I ask, repeating the question I'd asked Linda.

"Actually, surprisingly, little," he says. "Because my writing is mostly intellectually disciplined. I'm a student of history and I read mostly scholarly literature . . . so I have this intellectual sophistication that has kept much of that ridicule out of my life."

Remain disciplined, remain scholarly: these, he says, are the keys to retaining some sense of respectability in a field that receives so little of it.

His remark hits close to home: a reminder that to do otherwise is to make oneself vulnerable to the avalanche of ridicule sure to come.

"Remain disciplined and remain scholarly," I repeat. "That's good advice. Good advice for this whole project."

"Absolutely," he agrees, "and I don't doubt that you understand it and will proceed accordingly."

I nod into the phone, hopeful that he's right.

*

When dealing with the strange, it's best to proceed with caution, pumping the brakes with enough regularity to ensure that you're always in control. At least a little in control.

Which was surely a motivating factor in late April of 1961, when an open-minded Judge Carter wrote to NICAP director Major Donald Keyhoe, informing him of Joe Simonton's sighting and enclosing one of the three uneaten three-by-two-inch pancakes. His hope: that NICAP might chemically analyze the pancake to determine its ingredients' origins. Carter assumed NICAP would jump at the opportunity to prove or disprove the pancake's origin, but jump they did not. In fact, NICAP seemed to prefer to run in the opposite direction.

"As a body which sought to persuade scientists and middle-class professionals of the importance of the UFO problem, NICAP was known to be skittish about reports of UFO occupants," Jerry Clark wrote in his 1996 article on the Joe Simonton encounter. "NICAP did not want to be seen as a body engaged in the pursuit of 'little green men.'"

That the "men" Joe had encountered weren't actually green made little difference. They'd come bearing pancakes, after all, which seemed even more absurd to NICAP officials. Nonetheless, after receiving pressure from Judge Carter—a NICAP member himself—the organization felt compelled to do something. Begrudgingly, they agreed to test the pancake, though they urged Judge Carter to remain discreet about the organization's involvement. NICAP's reputation was at risk, NICAP secretary Richard Hall noted, and the peculiarity of the encounter seemed "ready-made for ridicule." Indeed, Joe Simonton's story had the potential for punditry written all over it. The convergence of plumber, pancakes, and space aliens seemed like a headline torn straight from the *National Enquirer*.

Which was bad news for NICAP, who for years had been making

steady strides toward increasing its credibility within the political sphere. So much so that by the spring of 1961, they were on the cusp of persuading Congress to hold hearings on the UFO phenomena. Hall feared that front page coverage of NICAP's role in investigating inter-planetary pancakes would surely distract, if not derail, their efforts.

"We do not propose to compromise [the potential hearings] for the sake of an unproven, and, you must admit, fantastic sounding claim," Hall informed Judge Carter.

Judge Carter found the reply nothing short of infuriating. Indeed, the claim was fantastic, which was precisely why he'd suggested a chemical analysis—to bolster or refute Joe's claims with scientific certainty. For Carter, NICAP's interest in preserving its reputation, even at the expense of greater truths, seemed an unforgivable trespass. They were on the doorstep of discovery, yet rather than knock on that door, NICAP preferred to slam it shut—or so Carter believed.

In his excoriating reply, Carter fired off a letter to NICAP director Major Donald Keyhoe, offering a defense of both Joe Simonton and himself.

"You are taking the position that it is up to Simonton to 'prove' his case. He has no Geiger instrument to prove that such a Radio Active Space ship hovered above his land; he has no funds to analyze the pancake." Carter went further to remind Major Keyhoe that the onus was on NICAP—the organization committed to investigating such claims—rather than the contactee. Joe Simonton had done his part by producing the pancakes (excluding the one he ate), and now it was up to NICAP to fulfill their charge.

Maybe Joe was "shack happy," Carter conceded. But there was only one way to find out.

*

Two years prior to Joe Simonton's encounter, Swiss psychologist and psychiatrist C. G. Jung published a short book titled *Flying Saucers*, which sought to explore the subject of UFOS "primarily as a psychological phenomenon." For skeptics, it seemed a worthwhile theory:

the notion that UFOs resided much closer than we ever imagined—in our own heads.

In his 1972 book, *The UFO Experience*, Dr. J. Allen Hynek offered his rebuttal. "If UFOs indeed are figments of the imagination, it is strange that the imagination of those who report UFOs from over the world should be so restricted."

Simply put, if UFOs are the product of our imaginations, then why aren't the descriptions of the crafts more imaginative? Why, in such varied instances, were witnesses describing much the same thing?

In the final chapter of his book, Jung plays devil's advocate to his own theory, arguing that there are "a good many reasons" why the UFO phenomena likely can't be limited to a psychological explanation alone. "So far as I know," Jung wrote, "it remains an established fact, supported by numerous observations, that UFOs have not only been seen visually but have also been picked up on the radar screen and have left traces on the photographic plate."

Leading one to wonder: Are our psyches somehow manifesting proof in the form of radar echoes, photographs, and pancakes? Or are we actually seeing saucers in the sky?

Perhaps the answer might lie in a third possibility, one which Jung himself explored: the possibility that 1950s Americans were simply projecting their "collective distress" in the form of UFOs.

Much as Sontag credited the Cold War for the apocalyptic tropes so often seen in sci-fi films, Jung suggested that America's diminishing relationship with the Soviets served as a likely cause for our "collective distress."

Were 1950s Americans seeing UFOs as a result of their inability to reckon with the threat of nuclear war? Were sightings of spaceships and "little green men" just another outlet to ease our anxieties?

*

After extensive testing by the Food and Drug Administration, it was determined that there was nothing to indicate that Joe Simonton's space pancakes were, in fact, otherworldly.

"Bacteriological examination and measurement of radioactivity gave results which are consistent with the view that the article is an ordinary pancake of terrestrial origin," reported the FDA.

I repeat: a pancake of *terrestrial* origin.

While microscopic analysis detected the presence of an array of ingredients—fat, starch wheat bran, as well as soybean and buckwheat hulls—nothing out of the ordinary was found.

NICAP's independent testing confirmed these results.

For most, this would seem the end of a long, strange chapter in UFO lore. But as is so often the case, when it comes to UFOs, the stories just get stranger.

Though the pancake's contents were proven to be of this world, who could say who—or what—had done the flipping? As some UFOlogists have suggested, it's possible that extraterrestrials simply cooked their pancakes from locally sourced food; that rather than lug a ship full of provisions through the universe, they replenished their supplies with Earth-grown materials.

Taken alongside the other oddities of this case, such a theory seems . . . dare I say logical?

That is, assuming you already agree with the premise that in 1961 three Italian-looking extraterrestrials flew their flying saucer to Eagle River, Wisconsin, handed off some pancakes to a guy named Joe, and then vanished into thin air.

It's a premise, I admit, about as hard to swallow as the pancakes.

*

With the physical evidence coming up short, the air force determined that Joe Simonton had simply experienced a close encounter of the hallucinatory kind. They reached this finding based on the assessment of a psychologist for the Aeronautical Systems Division who, as Jerry Clark pointed out, "neither met Simonton nor subjected him to formal psychological testing."

While any number of firsthand interviewers—including Hynek—vouched for Joe Simonton's sanity, it wasn't enough to dissuade the air force from drawing a different conclusion. Yet as Jerry Clark noted in his article, there were several complicating factors related to the air force's assessment, chief among them, how a hallucination could produce pancakes.

One possibility: because Joe had cooked them himself. Which he might have. After all, Joe freely admitted to having eaten pancakes for dinner the previous night. For some, such an admission only thickened the plot, though it proved nothing definitively. After all, having pancakes for dinner—though frowned upon in my waffle-leaning household— hardly makes a man mentally unsound.

Let's consider another theory: that Joe Simonton fabricated the story. Okay, but if so, then what might've motived him to do it?

During our phone interview, Jerry recounts that a friend once told him that he'd heard that Joe Simonton may have concocted the story as a means to "get back" at Judge Frank Carter.

"I said absolutely not," Jerry says. "That is extremely unlikely, a stupid theory concocted by someone who doesn't know anything about small town dynamics. One thing about living in a small, rural town: you keep your head down. You have to get along with your neighbors. You don't want them talking about you. If Simonton had a grudge against Judge Carter—and I don't know that he did, I've never read any real evidence that he did—he would not have concocted a flying saucer story, which would have put his head very high up there. You just don't do things like that in small towns."

For Jerry, the hoax theory simply doesn't pass the smell test.

"The whole story is just sort of odd and pointless," he says. "Usually the hoax stories have some point, some moral. They go somewhere. This doesn't go anywhere."

At its simplest, it's a story about a guy who ate a pancake. But at its most complicated, well . . . that's pretty complicated. With these com- plications come ever more complicated theories, a need to look beyond the singular event to see the larger story. And that story is never ending. There's always some new rock to look under, some new conclusion to draw. As Jerry and I discuss connections we've seen between various cases, I find myself hypothesizing one half-baked theory after another—all of which lack discipline and scholarship. Thankfully, Jerry knows to stop me in my tracks.

"You can always find some correlation when you look for it," he's quick to remind. "For example, there are patterns in UFO cases—there's no question about that—but you can also over read them. I think," he continues, measuring his words carefully, "that there's a lot of what might be called 'intellectual indiscipline.' And that's a kind way of putting it."

The less kind way of putting it involves words like "crackpot" and "pseudoscience."

However, "intellectual indiscipline" serves as the more collegial attempt at making the same point: that sometimes, in our haste, we jump to conclusions. Sometimes wholly unsupportable ones. In part, because—as we've discussed before—there's always some way to spin the facts toward our preferred hypothesis; some way to take individual stars in the sky and observe a constellation.

Though I've stopped short of running string between thumbtacks on a map of the world, some days I fear I haven't stopped that far short. For many, the idea of finding the key that unlocks all the mysteries of the universe is simply too enticing. What many fail to realize, however, is that there's no singular key for every lock that needs unlocking. Rather, we chip away at the mysteries of our universe one scientific theory at a time. And then, when science demands it, we revise those theories and start again.

Jerry admits that after a lifetime of researching and revising anomalous phenomena, he himself may not be much closer to the truth. "The problem is that we're dealing with things that are beyond current knowledge and maybe beyond imaginable knowledge," he explains. "Things that you did not think were important, just secondary and of marginal significance, can become of primary significance if you keep looking at it and reflecting on it. I look at my own thinking and it's just kind of gone in this big circle over the decades. Except that each time the circle turns out to be more intellectually sophisticated, more knowledgeable."

Despite this increase in sophistication and knowledge, it's still a circle, and a circle—like a hamster wheel—has no end.

"Is it frustrating," I ask, "knowing there might not be any great answers out there?"

"Oh, I don't expect to find answers," Jerry says. "What I expect to find is the process in which these experiences are undergone, and I think I've figured that out."

What he's discovered is that there are actually very few event anomalies in the world. Most anomalous events, Jerry claims, actually fall into the category of "high strangeness"; that is, encounters that are unprovable either as events or as illusions. Jerry's been collecting strange stories for decades, many of which were offered by sincere people of sound mind. "The problem is people just want to put it in a box, but really, it's happening in some liminal zone where things are both real and unreal at the same time. As I always say: real in memory and testimony but not in the world in the way that other things are real in the world."

Which is to say: we're most adept at experiencing our world on tangible terms. When you take away the tangible, we have a hard time even trusting ourselves.

*

Fifty-six years after Dr. Hynek's entrance into Eagle River, I make the trip myself, heading east from my home in Eau Claire until I see the Wisconsin River unfurl before me. I take a left, then wind down a tree-lined road until arriving at Joe Simonton's former property. The quaint, one-story house hardly looks like the scene of an alien encounter. As I slow my vehicle, I notice a vegetable garden out front, a small barn to the left of the house, and the swath of backyard where the spacecraft was alleged to have landed. I try to imagine Joe at the kitchen sink, his chickens clucking about in the yard, when a shimmer of silver caused him to glance up from his task.

On this day, the property's current owner is interrupted from his task as well, glancing at me from atop his ladder as he adds a fresh coat of paint to his detached garage. I'm startled by his presence, though the property owner seems completely nonplussed by my being there. I take a breath, then exit the vehicle and start a slow walk toward him.

"Hello there!" I call. The man turns to face me, and when it's clear I'm not leaving, he makes his way down the ladder.

I try to explain the situation, but it all comes out like babble. That I'm a professor working on a book about strange phenomena, and that a particularly strange event was alleged to have occurred on his property a little over half a century ago.

"I don't know if you've ever heard anything about it," I continue, "or if you're curious to learn more . . ."

He assures me that he's not.

"Oh, okay," I say, dumbfounded by his disinterest. "Well, it basically just involved a UFO . . . and some aliens . . . and some pancakes."

He doesn't even flinch.

"Anyway," I say. "I'll let you get back to your painting."

He returns to his place on the ladder.

As he walks away, I'm left wondering what's stranger: a man who claims to have received pancakes from space aliens, or a man who claims to have no interest in such a tale?

*

The following morning, as I prepare to leave Eagle River, I receive a call from lawyer Colyn Carter, the son of Judge Frank Carter, who'd believed Joe Simonton's story when few had. I'd reached out to Mr. Carter a month prior, leaving a phone message asking for a comment on his father's relationship with Joe. I'd been met with silence, leading me to believe that Colyn Carter had no comment to give.

I was wrong.

"I'm retired now," he explains. "But I came into the office today, saw your message, and I wanted to give you a ring."

"Do you mind if I swing by the office?" I ask.

"Come on over."

A moment later I'm driving back into town, parking before a non-descript office where Mr. Carter's practiced law for decades. I knock and am greeted at the door by eighty-year-old Colyn Carter, who shows me to a seat in his office.

"I just gave a talk on all this," Colyn says, handing me a manila file filled with newspaper clippings, as well as his own scrawled notes on yellow legal pages. "And no one at the talk knew anything about Joe or the pancakes," he continues. "I was the only one there who was in Eagle River back in 1961."

He was twenty-five then, a budding lawyer, and the son of the town's well-respected judge. What he remembers most about Joe Simonton's encounter is just how few people believed him.

"Some people knew Joe as the town drunk," Colyn explains candidly, "so they didn't take him seriously." In the beginning, Colyn didn't take him seriously either. It was simply easier to believe otherwise. "But the more I read over this," he continues, nodding to the folder of clippings, "the more I start to think otherwise."

According to Colyn, Joe's alleged propensity to drink, coupled with his description of the spacecraft's speed ("He said it flew off in two to three seconds!") raised more than a few eyebrows around town. "But my father believed him," Colyn continues. "He said there was no way Joe was going to gain from a hoax like this."

It made for an interesting odd couple—one of the most trusted men in town vouching for a man whose credibility didn't stretch nearly as far. But Judge Carter remained firm in his conviction, and long after the excitement of Joe's sighting wound down, the pair remained friends.

"[Joe's sighting] did a lot of good for the town," Colyn continues. "It brought all kinds of attention to Eagle River. People were writing Joe from Australia, from all over the world."

A month after his sighting, Joe confirmed that he'd received well over a thousand letters from interested strangers, an onslaught of correspondence that proved debilitating.

"And Joe, he was upset because he couldn't run his business anymore," Colyn continues. "All he wanted to do was get back to work."

"It seems strange to say given that we're talking about aliens and UFOS," I begin, "but . . . Joe seems like a pretty down to earth guy."

"You know, he was," Colyn confirms, "he really was."

Fifteen minutes later, I take my seat at a local restaurant, hungry for a late breakfast. Scanning the menu, my eyes soon fall to the pancakes. I smile.

As the waiter approaches, I consider asking him how they are, but of course I already know.

In Eagle River, there's only one answer to that question: the pancakes are out of this world.

CASE FILE #5

The Minot Air Force Base Sighting

October 24, 1968

NAME: THE MINOT AIR FORCE BASE SIGHTING

SCIENTIFIC NAME: N/A.

LOCATION: MINOT, NORTH DAKOTA

DESCRIPTION: IN THE EARLY MORNING HOURS OF OCTOBER 24, 1968, VAR-
IOUS AIR FORCE BASE CREWMEN AND A B-52 FLIGHT CREW OBSERVED
AN UNIDENTIFIED FLYING OBJECT IN THE SKIES IN AND AROUND THE
MINOT AIR FORCE BASE. IN ADDITION TO SEVERAL FIRSTHAND SIGHT-
INGS, THE UFO WAS ALSO PICKED UP ON THE RADARSCOPE ON BOARD
THE B-52 FLYING WITHIN THE SAME AIRSPACE.

WITNESS TESTIMONY: "I KNEW WHATEVER IT WAS THAT THERE WAS
SOMETHING THERE THAT I'D NEVER SEEN ON RADAR. I DON'T KNOW
OF ANYTHING THAT COULD GO LATERALLY IN THREE SECONDS, TWO
MILES, AND JUST STOP." CAPTAIN PATRICK MCCASLIN, 2001

CONCLUSION: UNSOLVED

At around 2:30 a.m. on October 24, 1968, Robert O'Connor and Lloyd
"Mike" Isley—a missile maintenance team stationed at Minot Air Force
Base in Minot, North Dakota—were driving south down a gravel road
toward a missile launch facility when they spotted a strange light in the sky.

Initially, O'Connor assumed it was a yard light left on by a local
farmer, though moments after drawing this conclusion, he revised it.

The light appeared to be moving. In fact, it appeared to be pacing
their truck.

Perhaps a helicopter, the men assumed, reaching for the radio to confirm it.

After a series of calls—Transportation Control transferred them to Base Operations and subsequently to Radar Approach Control (RAPCON)—it was determined that the skies were clear. Of helicopters, at least.

"Well," O'Connor replied, "there's something out here moving around."

They weren't the only ones who thought so. Fifteen minutes earlier, a security team about thirteen miles to the east had reported a similar sighting to their staff sergeant. O'Connor and Isley's sighting independently confirmed what the security detail had been observing: an unidentified flying object in the skies over Minot Air Force Base.

O'Connor and Isley's curiosity intensified as the bright light continued to pace them to a position south of their location, hovering in a manner inconsistent with the military aircraft they knew well.

"We arrived at the site and then started observing the object from outside the truck," Isley recalled. "It was moving in a large circular area to the south of us. It came within hearing distance twice. The sound was that of jet engines."

The men tracked the light as best they could, offering visual reconnaissance back to Base Operations and RAPCON, who eventually enlisted the help of a B-52 to investigate the matter from the air.

The order went to pilots Major James Partin and Captain Bradford Runyon, both of whom, along with their crew, had already logged over ten hours in the air as part of a routine combat training mission. Twenty-six-year-old Runyon was expecting an uneventful end to their run—a bit of upper air work before flying out to the "WT fix" position thirty-five miles northwest of the airbase. And finally, a smooth descent and landing.

But RAPCON's air controllers threw a wrench in the plan.

"And JAG31," the air controller radioed to Runyon at 3:35 a.m., "on your way out to the WT fix request you look out toward your 1:00 position for the next 15 or 16 miles and see if you can see any orange glows out there."

"Roger, roger . . . glow 31?" Runyon asked.

"Somebody is seeing flying saucers again," the air controller replied.

Perhaps due to hazy conditions, the crew observed no orange glows en route to the WT fix position. Yet as they began their turn back toward the runway, everything changed. It started when the B-52's radio transmitter began acting up. They could receive messages, but they were unable to send them. Something—or someone—appeared to be jamming the lines. And that's when Major Partin saw it: a "bright orange ball of light" directly off his one o'clock position.

"It appeared to be about 15 miles away, and either on the ground or just slightly above the ground," Major Partin reported. "The light remained stationary as we flew toward it."

The B-52's radar soon detected the unidentified craft in the air alongside them, worrying the crew that it might veer into their flight path. It didn't. Instead, it maintained a three-mile distance. Right up until—during a single, three-second sweep of the radar—it closed in to within a mile of the B-52. It was like magic: the blip was in one place and suddenly it was someplace else. The crew was dumbfounded. Even by today's standards, such a high-speed aeronautical maneuver is inconceivable.

Later analysis by intelligence office Staff Sergeant Richard Clark estimated that the unidentified object flew at an average velocity of 3,900 miles per hour, six times as fast as the B-52's top speed of 644 miles per hour.

"I knew whatever it was that there was something there that I'd never seen on radar," remarked Captain Patrick McCaslin, the crew's navigator. "I don't know of anything that could go laterally in three seconds, two miles, and just stop."

By then the craft had been spotted by multiple witnesses both on the ground and in the air, not to mention being picked up on the radarscope as well. Something was flying over the Minot skies. The problem was no one knew what.

Four minutes after the crew lost the ability to send outgoing radio transmissions, the UFO distanced itself from the B-52, at which point outgoing transmissions suddenly resumed.

When the control tower asked Runyon how far their aircraft had been from the UFO during the transmission blackout, he noted the craft had been within one and a half miles off their left wing.

"I wonder if that could have been your radio troubles," the control tower said.

"I don't know . . . but that's exactly when they started," Runyon said.

They landed the B-52 soon after.

Their mission was over. But the mystery had just begun.

*

Unlike most UFO encounters, the Minot sighting has no shortage of credible witnesses. So many, in fact, that researchers are faced with a unique problem: cobbling together a single, cohesive narrative by way of the various sets of eyes that bore witness to the event.

For over a decade, UFO historian Tom Tulien committed himself fully to untangling the mysteries of Minot. For him, it wasn't just a question of *what* it was, and *why* it was flying over Minot, but also: What's the intelligence behind it? Taken together, these answers held the potential to provide a much clearer picture of the 1968 Minot Air Force Base sighting, yet lacking those answers, the story remains as muddled as ever. In an effort toward achieving some clarity, from 2002 to 2012 Tom interviewed everyone he could associated with the encounter, compiling and curating his materials on a web page that offers the public unrestricted access to his findings.

I'd first learned about the Minot case, not due to Tom's online materials, but as a result of a conversation with eighty-three-year-old Bill McNeff, a chief investigator for the Minnesota chapter of the Mutual UFO Network. Over coffee one morning, I'd asked him about the "best" UFO cases he'd ever seen, and without hesitation, Bill pointed to Minot.

"It's the best one I've been close to," he told me.

Bill was clued into the case by way of his former brother-in-law, Staff Sergeant Richard Clark, who was stationed at Minot Air Force Base at the time of the sighting. Clark's specialty in radar analysis offered him unique access to the B-52 radarscope photographs, which had unequivocally captured something flying over the Minot skies that night. Curious about the unknown blip on the radarscope prints, Clark ordered two copies—one to be placed in a file folder on base, and another for himself. It was a fortuitous decision, one that allowed the radarscope prints to fall into the hands of Bill McNeff during a family gathering soon after.

Fast-forward thirty-five years, when, at the conclusion of a Mutual UFO Network meeting, Tom Tulien offhandedly mentioned to Bill that he was interested in studying the Minot case.

"Yeah?" Bill said. "Well I've got the radarscope prints."

Call it happenstance, call it fate—whatever you call it, thanks to Bill McNeff, Tom soon found himself in possession of some of the most valuable UFO evidence available. This wasn't just another eyewitness report, this was technologically acquired confirmable proof that an unknown craft had trailed a B-52 in the early morning hours of October 24, 1968.

No one knows this story better than Tom Tulien.

Which is why, one warm day in June, I park my car in front of his three-story rental property in Minneapolis. I make my way to the porch, studying the various doorbells until I see one marked "Tulien." I ring it, and moments later, sixty-two-year-old Tom hustles barefoot down the stairs, his long gray hair flowing behind him as he pulls the door wide, welcoming me into his home.

Though I've talked to dozens of folks in the UFO community, I'm intimidated by Tom. Not by the man himself, but by his vast knowledge of all things UFO. In addition to his decadelong study of the Minot case, he's also the founder of the Sign Oral History Project, a project committed to interviewing a wide range of people with knowledge of the UFO phenomenon: from government officials, to researchers, to firsthand eyewitnesses. Over the years, he's contributed thousands of transcribed pages to the effort, as well as overseen an online repository of primary and secondary UFO-related sources.

And much of this work has taken place in his living room.

"So this is my work station," Tom says, leading me to the third-floor room and nodding to several tables stacked high with papers and periodicals. Along the walls are several tan filing cabinets, as well as bookshelves dedicated primarily to UFO materials: back issues of Mutual UFO Network's *UFO Journal*, VHS tapes of UFO documentaries, among others.

"I've been meaning to clean all that up," Tom says, nodding to his desk. "Maybe someday . . ."

Maybe, indeed. Though I can't help but imagine that "tidying up" seems a rather low priority when one's tangling with the mysteries of the universe.

Tom and I take seats across from one another on his third-story deck, peering out at the eye-level tree line.

"Well, how can I help?" he asks.

For starters, by guiding a UFO newbie like me back to solid ground. A few months prior I'd entered into the subject of UFOs wide-eyed and open-minded, only to be taken hostage by the materials. I made the rookie mistake of delving too deep too quickly, churning through the information so rapidly that I became stricken by an acute case of UFO-induced vertigo. One internet search led to another, then another, until eventually the countless web pages of UFO reports began dragging me down like quicksand. None of it was disciplined. None of it was scholarly either. Weeks passed, and though I began experiencing sensations of "lost time," it had nothing to do with abduction. Rather, it was the result of being unable to look away. I'd convinced myself that the answer to our greatest cosmic mystery—"Are we alone here?"—was always just a few clicks away.

Trust me, it isn't. I've clicked.

In contrast to the endless array of opinion-based, poorly sourced UFO blogs I'd sifted through, Tom's Minot website provided some much-needed solid terrain. Here was a man who put scholarship over sensationalism, methodology over any need to find a Martian. The results speak for themselves—a carefully curated website complete with extensive endnotes and paper trail.

When I commend him on his work, he's quick to wave me off.

"You don't have to take my word for any of it," he says. "If you're reading a line in, say, section five, second paragraph, I always link to the source. You can go to an interview, or a document, and I'll link directly to where the source or claim comes from so readers can determine for themselves."

It's his "determine for themselves" philosophy that I find particularly appealing. Here's a guy who dedicated years of his life in pursuit of the truth rather than a quick paycheck.

"I'm not interested in promoting anything," he says. "I have nothing to promote. Nobody looks at my websites. The Minot site gets twenty hits a day if I'm lucky. And the Sign Oral History Project site gets a lot less, because it's specialized. But that doesn't bother me. I'm just interested in doing good work."

Because I, too, am interested in doing good work, I share with Tom my many concerns related to the subject matter. Specifically, how I fear that even "good work" on the subject of UFOs has the potential to prove insufficient given people's preference to roll their eyes rather than take a serious look.

"I was talking with a longtime UFOlogist recently," I tell Tom, "who more or less informed me that the only thing his research has ever brought him was grief."

"That's just part of the shtick, you know what I mean?" Tom says. "The thing is, a lot of time and energy has been put into creating ignorance around the subject. You can enter that ignorance, but you better be ready to deal with it on your own terms. Because it's not going to get you anything. It's not going to bring anything positive to your life."

Following his graduation from the Minnesota College of Art and Design in the late 1970s, Tom began actively seeking out positive experiences the world over, including a decadelong spiritual quest that included a five-month stint in a California monastery, where his intensive meditative practice helped him come to terms with reality and his role within it.

While there, he began feeling that there was a larger reality at work in the world, one not readily apparent. This reality, he thought, had something to do with advanced technologies such as UFOs, which the average person knew—and cared—little about.

After reading a four-volume set entitled *Message from the Pleiades: The Contact Notes of Eduard Billy Meier*—a staple within the UFO community—Tom's interest continued to grow. Though he didn't believe Swiss farmer Eduard Billy Meier actually shared an in-depth interaction with an extraterrestrial named Semjase as the books claim, he did believe there was an underlying truth to the material.

"There's a basis for truth in it, but I'm not sure what it is," Tom tells me. "But I do think it informs some sort of a larger thing."

Defining the "larger thing," however, has proven problematic. As our conversation veers toward local physics, consciousness, and dimensions beyond our own, I pause to take stock of our far-flung subjects. Though I've shared similar conversations while exploring the Mothman and the Beast of Bray Road, I'm hardly any better at them.

"It's so hard to talk about all this," I say, "because I feel like I don't know the right words. It all just ends up sounding a bit . . . crazy."

"It *is* crazy," Tom's quick to agree. "If you're limited to our present consciousness."

*

Google anything and you're bound to find something.

For instance, when I type "UFO Terrestrial Origin" into a search bar—more on that later—I receive nearly a million hits in just under a second. Then again, when I type the nonsensical "Cat Apricot Aquarius"—no more on that later, I swear—I get twice as many hits in the same amount of time.

Which goes to show that the universe is vast and mysterious, and so is the internet. And neither are terribly hospitable places to call home.

As Beast of Bray Road expert Linda Godfrey noted, for all its unvetted, unchecked, and patently false information, the internet, too, has done much for community building. While it may seem untoward to holler "I believe in UFOs!" in a crowded room, the UFO faithful have less trouble sharing their views in the virtual world.

Yet having already ventured down that particular rabbit hole, I find myself most at home with the curious skeptics who refuse to hide behind the safety of online anonymity. People like Tom Tulien, Linda Godfrey, Lon Strickler, Jerome Clark, among others, for whom the mystery remains. Yet they themselves are no mystery. By speaking publicly on these issues, they simultaneously enhance and risk their own credibility. They each have their theories, though they recognize, too, the limitations of them.

In the world of UFOs, one major limitation is a lack of quantitative "proof." Even in the rare instances when UFOlogists think they've at last uncovered something definitive, the scientific community regularly moves in to provide the often-damning counterpoint.

Nothing better epitomizes this push-and-pull than the oft-fraught relationship between UFO researcher and astrophysicist Dr. J. Allen Hynek (see: space pancakes) and famed astronomer and skeptic Carl Sagan (see: pretty much everything else on the subject of astronomy). While Hynek—a well-respected scientist in his own right—dedicated much of his life to UFO studies, Sagan dedicated a portion of his to discrediting what for him seemed like mere pseudoscience. It wasn't that Sagan doubted the existence of life in the universe, he simply hadn't seen any hard evidence to confirm it. Though he remained skeptical about UFOs, he was, in fact, optimistic about the possibility of life beyond Earth's borders. Sagan rightly demanded that the subject of UFOs undergo the same scientific rigor as any other subject, and though Hynek attempted to do just that, he often found his work relegated to popular publications such as the *New Yorker* and the *Saturday Evening Post*, rather than the more scientifically trusted peer-reviewed journals. While publishing in such widely read magazines helped steer the subject of UFOs away from the fringes and into the mainstream, it also gave scientists ammunition to criticize Hynek and others like him whose research hadn't endured the muster of peer review.

For Hynek, it was quite the catch-22. The majority of peer-reviewed journals wanted nothing to do with his research, yet he was faulted for not publishing in them.

In 1967—likely to the ire of some of his scientist colleagues—he published in yet another mainstream magazine, *Playboy*. The following year, Hynek received a letter from a young boy whose father had shared the article with him (albeit, minus the centerfold). In a moment of candor, Hynek offered his thoughts on the problems of publication venues.

"I am glad your father removed my article from *Playboy* to show it to you," Hynek wrote. "It is unfortunate that *Playboy* was willing to publish this article but *Scientific American* was not. This is a sad commentary on the closed-mindedness of many scientists."

Close-mindedness, perhaps, or maybe just a means of self-preservation. By the 1960s scientists were acutely aware of the stigma surrounding UFO research. In her book *The Lure of the Edge*, author Brenda Denzler notes that a 1952 survey of astronomers confirmed that not a single one would "admit publicly to having an interest in UFOs." The interest was there—"fear of public ridicule did not prevent scientists from having a privately respectful interest in the subject," Denzler writes—though offering a public acknowledgment of one's interest was all but unheard of, particularly within academic circles.

In the military, too, speaking on the record about UFOs had the potential to damage one's career. Copilot Bradford Runyon admitted to remaining tight-lipped about what he'd seen in the Minot skies because he "had a pretty good military career right then" and "didn't want to jeopardize that."

In the golden age of UFO sightings, the idiom from World War II propaganda posters had taken on new relevance: loose lips, sink ships.

But they could also sink careers.

*

Tom Tulien's the first to admit that some of his ideas are indeed "out there," though he knows the truth is out there, too—obscured as it may be. And after a decade's worth of work related to the Minot case, he's become rather certain that the "truth" related to UFOs may actually have little to do with aliens.

"I'm convinced that at the core of it, there's a technology involved, and I'm not convinced it's from off planet."

Translation: UFO technology may have a *terrestrial* origin, developed by humans right here on Earth. And if not developed by humans, then perhaps reverse engineered from alien technologies that have found their way into human hands—a scenario akin to an extraterrestrial Prometheus handing the proverbial fires over to man. Though Tom doesn't buy into the "reverse engineering" theory, he's more than willing to accept what to him seems obvious: that these unknown crafts were built by humans.

This theory certainly spurs a new way of thinking on the matter. I'd always naively assumed that UFOs and extraterrestrials went hand-in-hand, that the so-called Martians were the ones in the drivers' seats of the crafts.

Not necessarily, Tom says.

"Let me get this straight," I say, buying myself time for this new information to sink in. "You're drawing a distinction between extraterrestrials and UFOs?"

"Exactly. And that's always been the problem," Tom says. "In fact, that's been the government's goal, I could argue. To make it appear as though UFOs are *alien* spacecraft because then nobody pays attention to it."

"So discrediting the UFO phenomenon by hitching it to a phenomenon even more difficult to swallow?"

Tom nods.

More threatening than the existence of extraterrestrial life, he explains, is the existence of a human-made technology that cannot be easily measured and metered. If the general population had access to whatever energy source might be powering UFOs, Tom says, then the world economy would have to be reimagined.

"It's a technology ahead of its time," Tom says, "and there's been a lot of effort spent creating ignorance around the subject to keep it out of the public's consciousness."

Suddenly my notion of "little green men" is replaced by who I imagine must be the "true" culprits: shadow governments, leaders of the military complex, and God knows who else. It's a storyline snagged straight from the *X-Files*—complete with a Cigarette Smoking Man, hollow-eyed denizens of world domination, among other nefarious powerbrokers.

As I try to keep my head from spinning, Tom hits me with another head-spinner.

"There is no evidence of aliens that I know of," he says matter-of-factly, a statement I never expected to hear from a man so committed to the subject. Make no mistake: Tom is convinced that there are intelligently controlled, unconventional flying objects in the sky; he simply questions who's piloting them.

It's a question that's only intensified for Tom over time. For decades, he's collected countless stories involving alien contact and abduction, all of which he's ultimately found unrewarding. "There's no way of objectively verifying stuff like that," he says. "You can at least do work on UFO cases that have data, such as the Minot case, which is data rich. If you read about it and study it enough you come to a point where you have quite a bit of information to coalesce that allows you to convince yourself one way or another."

Data is the key, he explains. Without it, all you're left with is a story.

Yet in the Minot case, even the story serves as important evidence. Particularly when the story is told by firsthand witnesses, many of whom were highly trained military personnel, and some of whom had top secret clearance. These were people entrusted to oversee ICBM missiles in the midst of the Cold War, people our country had come to rely upon.

Which is not to say their stories synced up perfectly. Indeed, there were slight variations related to time and distance and coloration of the craft, though several consistent through lines remained.

"There was something there, there's no question," Tom tells me. The difficulty is concluding what precisely that "something" was.

"I know one theory is that it was a ball of plasma," I begin. "Similar to ball lightning."

"A ball of plasma?" Tom scoffs. "There's no such thing as a ball of plasma that's free floating and pacing an airplane for four minutes."

Moreover, Tom tells me, plasma is generally the size of a grapefruit and is often spotted near the ground rather than several thousand feet above it.

"But let's imagine that what occurred at Minot *was* a plasma event," Tom says. "If so, that's the first time it's ever happened, it's never been observed since, and it'll probably never be observed again. Shouldn't that be of interest to science? Shouldn't that be the primary interest of a plasma physicist or someone who studies lightning or electrical storms?"

I find myself nodding.

"And yet there's absolutely no interest," Tom says. "If it's plasma as they say it is, then that's as profound as a UFO."

The "they" refers to the Project Blue Book team—an office once housed in Wright-Patterson Air Force Base near Dayton, Ohio. Their mission, as previously noted, was to investigate UFO sightings. Preferably quickly.

In Project Blue Book's final report on the Minot case, Lieutenant Colonel and Blue Book director Hector Quintanilla relied heavily on the plasma theory to explain the radarscope photographs and radio loss. Quintanilla further complicated Blue Book's findings by suggesting that the star Sirius might account for what witnesses on the ground claimed to have seen. For many, it seemed a tenuous conclusion, and one that was reached in a remarkably fast turnaround time of under three weeks.

Why plasma? Why ball lightning? Of all the possible explanations, why rely upon such obscure weather phenomena?

For Tom, the reason's obvious. And it's the same reason ball lightning has regularly served as the go-to explanation to dismiss a UFO sighting, particularly in the 1960s.

"Because we didn't know what ball lightning was back then," Tom tells me. "It was a perfect explanation: an unknown for an unknown."

Project Blue Book was in the business of finding answers to the unknowns—or at least offering the perception that the air force was committed to such a cause. But "finding answers" isn't the same as "creating closure," and the latter is likely a more accurate description of Project Blue Book's true intentions—work it carried out by debunking as many sightings as it could any way it could.

Tom isn't alone in his dismissiveness toward Project Blue Book's findings. Many within the UFO community and beyond have concluded that the project was little more than a public relation's arm of the air force, an official mechanism for dismissing the array of sightings that occurred between 1952 and 1969. At times as few as three people were assigned to the project, making it difficult to conduct legitimate and comprehensive reviews amid sorely stretched resources. Which was perhaps by design.

"Nobody wanted to work there," Tom tells me. "It was an insult to work there because everyone knew it was a joke."

At least the people with the clearance to be in on the joke.

As Project Blue Book's explanations became more difficult to swallow, Dr. J. Allen Hynek, who himself was once a scientific consultant for the project, began questioning the project's scientific rigor. Following the many outlandish UFO explanations he'd heard (and had previously propagated, including the eye-roll-inducing swamp gas theory), Hynek believed that under Quintanilla's leadership, "the flag of the utter nonsense school was flying at its highest on the mast."

As a result, in Tom's view, Project Blue Book's investigation of the Minot sighting was doomed from the start. "The majority of Minot Air Force Base was under nuclear clearances," Tom explains. "The only people who gave testimony on the UFO case didn't have top secret clearance."

In short, according to Tom, the people who had the most information to offer were never interviewed by Project Blue Book investigators. Thirty-two years later, Tom began interviewing the people Project Blue Book hadn't—the B-52 crew members, among various observers on the ground. In doing so, he pieced together an account that proved far more complicated than Blue Book's explanation of a star and some plasma or ball lightning.

Despite all Tom's learned throughout this intensive interview process, he still remains firm that firsthand accounts can never serve as definitive proof.

"Anecdotes are never enough," he tells me. "That's too easy. You can interpret it anyway you want. I want some restrictions on how you interpret something. And the only way you get that is by combining primary evidence."

The interviews are important, he agrees, but they become more so when the interviewees' stories align with the paper trail. To understand the Minot case fully one needs to immerse oneself in the data, stew around for a while, and then take a good hard look at the context, the motives, and the facts.

"That's what I've done for the past ten years," Tom says, "just immersing myself in data. I was as confused as everyone else for years."

Eventually the facts converged enough to allow him to draw a few conclusions, including his belief that an intelligent craft of terrestrial origin flew through the Minot sky that night.

Yet he acknowledges, too, that this theory—and all his theories—are based on the facts he understands to be true, facts that might ultimately betray him. As a self-trained historian, Tom's cognizant of the risks inherent in trusting one fact over another. But for him, the rewards outweigh those risks.

"History is choosing the significant from the insignificant," Tom says. "And the Minot case is not just a UFO case. It has the potential to teach how history is done, what its limits are, what it can say and what it can't say. It's all there." Tom learned these lessons throughout his decadelong study, a painstakingly meticulous process that ultimately taught him how to think critically, analyze, and share data in a responsible way. Though the field of UFOlogy is overrun with unknowns, Tom prefers the facts—few as they are.

In December of 1969—after twenty-two years of fact-finding and 12,618 investigations—the air force discontinued Project Blue Book once and for all. Its final report offered three conclusions related to the UFO phenomenon.

First, the air force did not believe UFOs to be a threat to national security.

Second, the air force saw no evidence that UFOs demonstrated "technological developments or principles beyond the range of present day scientific knowledge."

And finally, no evidence confirmed that sightings designated as "unidentified" were "extraterrestrial vehicles."

While Tom would surely take issue with the second finding (given their speed and maneuverability, how could UFOS *not* demonstrate new developments in scientific knowledge?), their third finding justifies his own. If Project Blue Book was correct that no evidence indicated that the sightings were "extraterrestrial vehicles," might they be terrestrial in origin?

"Let's say they are terrestrial," Tom says. "If so, then the air force is perfectly consistent in their answer. 'We have this under control and they're not a threat to our national security.' All I'm saying is once you plug in the idea that the technology *is* terrestrial, and you go back through the history, it makes sense in a new way. If its extraterrestrial, that makes sense in that way, but if it's our intelligence, then it makes sense in another way."

A way that implies that our government knows a lot more than its willing to tell us.

"The fact is truth can't be eradicated," Tom says. "And you need to know the truth in order to deceive."

*

Some UFO sightings—like Joe Simonton's space pancakes encounter—lend themselves to a bit of levity. But the Minot case does not. Try as I might, it's hard to crack a joke given the UFO's proximity to missile silos, not to mention the indisputable radarscope photos. Little green men are one thing, but how do we laugh upon learning that we humans might be the source of this particular mystery? That the threat is potentially made by us and aimed at us?

As our conversation winds down, neither Tom nor I are in a jovial mood. I check my watch to learn I'm experiencing even more "lost time"—the afternoon having somehow gotten away from us. Admittedly, our conversation has strayed quite a way from Minot, North Dakota; such is the nature of the strange. But to my mind, Tom and I've moved beyond radarscope photos and missile silos in an effort to plum toward a deeper truth: one teetering perilously close to the limits of our knowledge.

And the limits, too, of what we *want* to know.

"If there's one thing this subject has taught me it's how ignorant we are," Tom says. "It's what this whole thing's about. That's what our political situation is about right now, too: ignorance. And taking advantage of ignorance. And promoting ignorance."

In some ways, we're back to where we started: Tom's frustration with a populace unwilling to engage in big questions for fear of the big answers that might emerge. And a populace, too, that frowns upon those who try.

"How do you fix it?" I ask.

"You don't," he says, looking me straight in the eyes. "You do it for yourself."

But given the high risk, low reward nature of the subject matter, I'm not at all convinced I want to.

"At this point," Tom says, "I have no hopes that in my lifetime anyone will ever pay attention to this or put in as much dedication as I have. If there were other cases out there as qualified as this to investigate, I'd transition to those right away. But I haven't found one yet that is that enthralling."

Tom agrees with Bill McNeff that the Minot sighting is the highest quality case he's seen, though he's quick to dismiss the possibility that Minot alone holds the key to unlocking the mysteries of the UFO phenomenon.

"But if there were six [sightings] like this, can you imagine?" he asks.

Even astronomer, astrophysicist, and famed UFO debunker Donald Menzel held a much lower threshold for truth, noting that if a *single* sighting "with irreproachable credentials and inescapable significance" was discovered, then, "the reality of nature of the UFO phenomenon would be established."

Carl Sagan, too, asked for just one solid case.

"I predict," Sagan told Hynek, "that if and when you ever get a really good case that involves hard evidence, there will be no lack of federal funds."

But is Minot that case? And are radarscope photos the "hard evidence" Sagan called for?

Maybe Minot's unique due to the residual evidence, or maybe it's due to Tom's scholarly approach to examining it. After all, his fact-driven assessment serves as a model for how UFO sightings might be examined through a more disciplined and scholarly lens.

Which, aside from the need for more quantitative evidence, is perhaps the largest missing piece of this puzzle: how to create a clear and consistent methodology to study the sightings.

Consider the magnitude of Tom's task: not only is he trying to explain an unexplained phenomenon, but he's doing so while developing a methodology worthy of scientific rigor.

"The problem is there's nothing to grasp," he says.

Though new to the field, it's a phenomenon I already know well: just when you think you're gaining traction, that traction slips away. It's an important reminder of the nature of facts; they're only as valuable as the rigor they endure.

Force the facts to confront that rigor, Tom argues, echoing Sagan. Then let the truth fall where it may.

*

A few weeks after talking with Tom, I place a call to Lloyd "Mike" Isley, who, along with Robert O'Connor, was among the first to report the sighting to Base Operations all those years ago.

At seventy-one, the all-but-retired air conditioning technician still vividly recalls what he saw in the sky in the early morning hours of October 24, 1968. He was twenty-three, fresh out of tech school, and thrust suddenly into the military world. Though studying air conditioning repair seems a far cry from the kind of training needed to ensure the stability of Minuteman missiles, not so, according to Mike. He and half a dozen others worked in the refrigeration shop in their squadron, doing their part to ensure that the missiles were kept at the appropriate temperature. The missiles' stability depended upon it. Most of their work took place in the soft support buildings adjacent to the missile silos, one of which he and O'Connor were driving toward on the morning of the sighting.

Throughout our interview, Mike confirms much of what I'd heard before: how the farmer's light transformed into a helicopter before transforming again into something without a name. And how Base Control was compelled enough by his and O'Connor's sighting to send in a B-52 for closer inspection.

Mike explains how he and O'Connor exited the truck alongside the soft support building, then watched the strange light for several more minutes before the B-52 thundered overhead, seeming to take the light with it.

"Were you scared?" I ask.

"I was somewhat scared," Mike says in his Oklahoman drawl. "You know, not knowing whether the thing was going to land or drop something on us or whatever. I wasn't real calm, you know, but I wasn't ready to jump in the truck and make a run for it or anything."

After completing a "Sighting of Unidentified Phenomena Questionnaire," Mike returned to his normal duties. A few nights passed, at which point he and O'Connor had a chance to chat about what they'd seen over the Minot sky. In many respects, Mike's version of events synced with Robert O'Connor's, though their stories differed on a few key points: including time of night and the details regarding what exactly they saw.

"I'll put it this way," Mike chuckles, "O'Connor saw a lot more detail in the thing than I saw."

The sighting wasn't mentioned again. That is, until Mike was contacted by Tom Tulien in 2001, when he learned there was more to the story than he initially knew.

Four years later, in 2005, journalist Peter Jennings hosted a show on ABC titled *UFOs: Seeing Is Believing*. In the months leading up to production, a producer reached out to Mike to hear his account of the Minot sighting.

"I basically told them the same thing I told you, and I think it maybe cost me a shot at being able to be on TV," he laughs.

Mike's best guess for what he saw that night dovetails neatly with Tom's theory: an experimental aircraft of terrestrial origin.

"Either that or it was a visitor from another planet or something," he says. "A lot of people think that out of all the millions and billions of planets there's got to be another one that's probably more advanced than we are. And that wouldn't surprise me."

"No?" I ask.

"It wouldn't surprise me if there were visitors from another planet or something," he confirms, though he doesn't believe any otherworldly visitors flew over Minot on the night in question.

"I'm open-minded about it," he says. "If somebody could give me good proof that it was a visitor from outer space I'd believe it, or a Russian vehicle or something. I'm open to suggestions."

As am I. Which is why, as my search winds down, I reach out to Minot Air Force Base for their take on the matter.

I'm not sure what I expect. Perhaps to receive duplicative information from Tom's site: the internal memos, the radarscope photos, the Project Blue Book report.

What I get, instead, is a response from the base spokesperson informing me that Minot Air Force Base's archives and history office have nothing to support the UFO claims.

Nothing? But what about all the documentation Tom's acquired?

The spokesperson clarifies that Minot Air Force Base isn't necessarily denying the event itself, the base simply doesn't serve as the repository for the paperwork related to the claim. It's an information management issue, hardly the conspiracy theory I'd imagined. The spokesperson refers me to a few other places to look for further information (none of which do me much good) before informing me that as far as Minot Air Force Base is concerned, the case is officially closed.

As are most of the Project Blue Book cases; their job, after all, was to close them.

Not to mull over the mystery, or consider the possibilities, but to give each sighting a worldly explanation.

Call it a star, plasma, ball lightning. Call it anything but a UFO.

The Val Johnson Incident

August 27, 1979

NAME: THE VAL JOHNSON INCIDENT

SCIENTIFIC NAME: N/A

LOCATION: MARSHALL COUNTY, MINNESOTA

DESCRIPTION: SHERIFF'S DEPUTY VAL JOHNSON WAS ON PATROL NEAR STEPHEN, MINNESOTA, IN THE EARLY MORNING HOURS OF AUGUST 27, 1979, WHEN HE SPOTTED A STRANGE LIGHT IN THE SKY. WITHIN SECONDS, THE LIGHT WAS INSIDE THE SQUAD CAR, LEAVING PHYSICAL EVIDENCE ON BOTH THE CAR AND JOHNSON HIMSELF.

WITNESS TESTIMONY: "IT FELT LIKE I GOT HIT IN THE FACE WITH A TWO-HUNDRED-POUND PILLOW. AND THAT'S THE LAST I RECALL."

VAL JOHNSON, 2017

CONCLUSION: UNSOLVED

At around 2:00 a.m. on August 27, 1979, thirty-five-year-old Sheriff's Deputy Val Johnson peered out the window of his 1977 Ford LTD cruiser to spot a strange light in the sky.

"I thought maybe a semi hit a deer," Val tells me thirty-eight years later, as we huddle over our coffees at Perkins Restaurant, "or maybe an aircraft with one of those big lights had landed there."

I nod, taking a long sip of coffee to keep from pinching myself. After all, it's not every day you get to sit across the table from Val Johnson of "Val Johnson Incident" fame. A man whose run-in with an unidentified

Fig. 10. Val Johnson of the Val Johnson Incident, 2018. Courtesy of the author.

flying object was, according to anomalist Jerry Clark, "one of the top 10 most influential UFO encounters in history."

I'd been researching Val's sighting for a couple of weeks before learning the most important detail of all: that Val was rumored to live right up the road from me in Eau Claire, Wisconsin.

Fingers crossed, I fired off a letter, and within two days, received a reply.

Good morning! Val wrote. *I would be pleased to meet with you at Perkins Restaurant. . . . Perkins has a "back room" which is somewhat private and I think we could possibly be quite secure there. Let's hope for suitable seating.*

Quite secure? Suitable seating?

What does he think might happen to us at a Perkins on a Thursday morning? I'd wondered.

Though the answer—as Val Johnson knows all too well—is that anything has the potential to happen anywhere.

From the edge of my seat, I listen as the salt-and-pepper-bearded seventy-two-year-old gives me the play-by-play. He leans forward in the booth, his checkered flannel shirt stretching across his broad shoulders as he returns to that summer night all those years ago.

"I was pretty new," he says, "I'd only been a field officer for a couple of months when I saw it." Yet no amount of experience could've ever prepared him for what took place that night.

Though of course the night began like any other: quiet and uneventful. Boasting a population just over thirteen thousand, Marshall County, Minnesota, was hardly a hotbed for criminal activity. Excluding the occasional traffic violation, nights, for Val, were mostly about passing the time. The mundane nature of the job was reflected in the landscape—a terrain so wide and flat that, as Val put it, "If you get up on a stepladder on a Wednesday you can see both Sundays."

But even without the ladder, on August 27, Val saw more than he'd bargained for.

His shift started nearly nine hours prior, at around 5:00 p.m., when he put on his uniform, waved goodbye to his family, and slipped into the rust-colored cruiser he kept in the drive. He was scheduled for a power shift, which usually ran until 3:00 or 4:00 a.m. Over the previous months he'd grown accustomed to the long, late hours, whittling them away by frequenting various diners to chat with locals. In towns like Marshall, part of an officer's duty involved being present, and what better way to make oneself known than by going where the people were?

But eventually the diners ran out, the people returned home, and Val had no choice but to endure the solitude of another quiet night on patrol.

By 1:00 a.m., as the clock wound down, so too did the fuel gauge in his cruiser. Val pulled into a gas station in the nearby town of Stephen. The station had been closed for hours, though in towns of that size, it was customary to provide law enforcement a key in the event officers needed to refuel after hours. Val made good use of his key that night, topping off the tank as he stared into the silent, windswept darkness. Returning the nozzle to its holder, Val settled in for the last few hours of his shift. He buckled up, then headed west on County Road 5 back toward his home in the town of Oslo.

That's when he spotted the glow emanating in a southwesterly direction several miles off. It might've been anything—the aforementioned semi or aircraft, among other possibilities. His curiosity piqued, Val pressed down hard on the accelerator, closing in at a speed between fifty to sixty miles per hour. At first, the light was merely a welcome distraction, through as he drove toward it, he soon realized that it was much more than just that. The light had no apparent source, Val realized. There was no semi, no aircraft, no easy explanation for what he saw.

"And then," Val tells me, snapping his fingers, "just like that, the light was in the car with me."

It soon overpowered him: a burst of light so fast and so great that he had no time to react. It pinballed around the interior of his car like a Roman candle, the bright flash momentarily blinding him.

"It felt like I got hit in the face with a two-hundred-pound pillow," Val continues, raising his hands to reenact the scene. "And that's the last I recall."

For the next thirty-nine minutes or so, Val lay unconscious in his car. When at last he woke, he found his cruiser positioned sideways in the northbound lane of the road—the engine off, but the headlights still cutting beams into the dark.

For Val, the world reemerged in slow motion. As he widened his eyes he was soon overcome with a burning sensation rippling across his face. Instinctually, he thrust his hand toward his radio and called for assistance.

"What is your condition?" the dispatcher asked.

"I don't know. Something just hit my car," Val replied. "I don't know . . . Strange."

An off-duty officer from Stephen was the first to arrive on the scene. Speeding through the night, he eventually spotted the unmoving cruiser on Highway 220. He pulled to the side of the road to find Val leaning against the steering wheel. A disoriented Val described to the officer an intense burning sensation spreading across his eyes and face, at which point the officer ensured that Val was transported to a nearby hospital, where doctors attempted to soothe the burns with ointments and bandages. He was conscious though rattled, and at a complete loss to make sense of the encounter.

At some point between 3:00 and 4:00 a.m. a fellow deputy drove Val back to the station, where he recorded a statement of the night's proceedings. As he concluded his statement, it occurred to him that he ought to call his wife, who'd surely be worried as a result of his late arrival. His eyes still bandaged, Val stretched out his arm and asked the deputy beside him to read the time on his watch. The deputy did, revealing a time fourteen minutes slow. Curious, the deputy checked the dashboard clock on Val's cruiser to find it running fourteen minutes behind as well. It seemed an unlikely coincidence given that both clock and watch had been running perfectly throughout his shift.

Where did those fourteen minutes go? Val wondered. *And how could two independent timekeeping devices manage to lose them?*

The plot thickened further as law enforcement began detailing the physical damage left behind on the cruiser: a cracked windshield, a dented hood, a broken headlight, and two stainless steel antennas bent to ninety-degree angles.

Whatever had hit the car had left its mark, and with it, a treasure trove of physical evidence. Hence, Jerry Clark's "top 10" designation.

Between the abrasions on Val's body, the damage to the car, and the fourteen lost minutes, the sheriff's department of Marshall County had a mystery on its hands—the likes of which they'd never seen.

It was one thing for a citizen to report a strange light in the sky, but quite another for a trusted sheriff's deputy to have the evidence etched on his skin.

*

If you've read this far, by now you know the truth: we humans just aren't wired for the weird. Or at least not the mystery that often accompanies it.

According to Donna Webster and Arie Kruglanski's 1996 article "Motivated Closing of the Mind," not only do we need closure, but we prefer to receive it quickly (the "urgency tendency") and indefinitely (the "permanence tendency"). However, as the researchers make clear, such tendencies come with consequences. "People under a heightened need for closure may seize on information appearing early in a sequence and freeze on it, becoming impervious to subsequent data."

Translation: once we get an idea in our heads, it's hard to get it out of our heads.

Yet thirty-eight years after the incident, Val confirms that he's never really settled upon any singular idea for what he experienced that night. Closure was a luxury he never received. Instead, following the incident, he simply tried to get on with his life, leaving the theorizing to others. Even today, all he knows for certain was that he saw *something*, though he refuses to give that something a name.

"You must have a few theories," I press.

He mulls it over, staring deep into his coffee.

"In police work," he begins, "you take a series of evidentiary findings and you put them in a line and you come up with a conclusion. In my particular instance, you take two of those and line them up, the third is not there, or the third disproves the second. Nothing lines up. Nothing makes sense. *Nothing* makes sense," he repeats. "Consequently, there's been a great deal of conjecture trying to come up with a viable solution or a viable explanation. It's not there."

But not for a lack of evidence. After all, we've got the windshield, the dents, the burns, the lost time, and when compiled and analyzed, the answer couldn't be clearer: what we're dealing with is one heck of a mystery.

My answer is as unsatisfying as the one the sheriff's department reached at the end of their own investigation. Other than to acknowledge that the vehicle had been involved "in an accident with an unknown object," the report offered little speculation as to what that "unknown object" might've been. It was a pragmatic choice, even if it lacked alluring details. But there were reputations to consider, and in Marshall County, one's reputation mattered. If the sheriff's department's report had dared used the phrase "unidentified flying object," it's hard to imagine the extent of the consequences. Even the phrase they eventually settled upon—"unknown object"—was likely a risk, though less of one than the highly charged acronym UFO.

Baffled by the statement set forth by his deputy, the morning following the incident, Marshall County Sheriff Dennis Brekke picked up the phone and called Allan Hendry, chief investigator for the Center for UFO Studies in Chicago. Upon hearing the details of the incident, Hendry agreed to investigate the matter personally. He descended upon Marshall County, dedicating days to in-depth interviews and an examination of the physical evidence left behind on the car.

His findings: inconclusive.

"Hoax doesn't seem very likely in this case," Hendry explained. "Not only for all that Johnson's colleagues and friends have said about the man, but because of the unusualness of the effects."

Not only was the damage to Val and the cruiser undeniable, but it was unexplainable, too.

"The biggest mystery about the Val Johnson case to me," Hendry remarked, "is to try to find one neat explanation for something that could behave the way he described, yet could create the kinds of damage that we analyzed and discovered."

Other experts were called in as well, including Meridan French, a glass specialist from the Ford Motor Company, who himself traveled to Marshall County to examine the cruiser's windshield. After a thorough examination, French concluded that he couldn't pinpoint the cause of the fractured windshield, noting that he believed it was "not of the ordinary in nature."

"I'm convinced that the fractures as we see here were made by some type of a blow from the outside of the glass by some firm, probably hard object," French explained. The object did not have "sufficient force to crush the glass," he continued, "but enough force to bend the glass to the point of breaking it."

Which was "extremely unusual" he admitted, and unlike anything he'd ever seen.

For many, the mystery was unnerving, though for Val, it was simply a fact of life. "For the first three years it was on my mind daily," he tells me. "After that I went on with my life, had more children, other jobs, and got busy doing this, that, and the other. It's of no great concern to me at this point."

"You just chalked it up as a mystery and moved on?" I ask.

He nods, turning his attention to his newly arrived cinnamon roll.

"It's not a defining incident in my life."

It would be for others. Not only did Val's encounter complicate people's worldviews, but it empowered many to come forward with their own unbelievable tales.

"I had a plethora of visitors," Val says, "of various psychological stripes."

For years, his backyard picnic table in Oslo, Minnesota, became a meeting place for those who'd experienced the strange. Over lemonade, Val's visitors recounted their tales, while also offering theories for what Val may have encountered. Without exception, Val nodded politely, smiled, and thanked them for their time.

"And that's as far as any of that ever went," Val says. "I did not buy into any prepacked scenario. You come to my house, you want to talk about this, you drove all the way from Wichita to talk to me, great. Let's have lemonade and talk about it."

But he was careful never to encourage them. And careful, too, to protect his own credibility. Though the latter had become increasingly difficult given that his name had become synonymous with the strange—a stain that followed him wherever he went. Ever since his early morning encounter in 1979, Val Johnson had been forced to become Val Johnson of the "Val Johnson Incident." Indeed, that's how I initially knew him: not as a hardworking husband and father, but as the man who once saw a light in the sky. I'd done what we of the twenty-first century so often do: boiled down a life into a moment. And in the case of Val Johnson, a moment hardly representative of the man himself.

For decades, Val has dutifully lugged the baggage that accompanied his encounter, though after a few years, the limelight began to fade. Which was fine by Val, who was anxious to return to normal life.

Aware of this, I measure my next words carefully, fearful that by even broaching the topic, I risk exposing him once more to a world he's been slow to embrace.

"The words we haven't brought up yet—and a lot of folks have in terms of this experience—are 'UFO' or 'extraterrestrial.' Are you distancing yourself from those possibilities?"

"They're possibilities," he agrees. "It could be a UFO. It could be extraterrestrial. It could be time travel. It could be top secret military from Grand Forks Air Force Base. It could be a variety of things. But my pay grade does not permit me to make all these speculations with any credibility. So I don't."

For Val, it simply is what it is: a mystery. And he's content leaving it at that.

But not me. I need closure, even if Val doesn't. If not the answer as to what he saw on August 27, 1979, then at least some sense of what the encounter meant to him.

"This whole experience," I begin, "has it been a blessing or a curse?"

"It has not negatively impacted me at all," Val says. "There have been people who questioned my sanity, you know, at the very beginning. They said, 'Why is he saying this? Why is he doing this?' So I came right out and I told them: 'I'm not running for public office, I don't have vitamins to sell you, there's nothing. This is what happened to me. If you choose to believe, great. If you choose not to believe, that's okay too. I'm not selling anything.'"

Val's indifference proves persuasive. If most folks are motivated by fame or fortune, I'm impressed by the degree to which Val appears disinterested in both. Except for an unsolicited $1,000 check from the *National Enquirer* for "Best UFO Story of the Year," Val tells me he hasn't earned a penny as a result of his encounter.

As for his "fame"—some might call it infamy—it was, indeed, short-lived. In the coming weeks, Val's story soon gave way to others, drifting from the headlines and filed under "the unexplained." Aside from the UFO faithful, the incident was mostly forgotten. Though for years, Val continued to find himself on the receiving end of the occasional phone call or visit from strangers, some more unusual than others.

Particularly strange was a conversation he had with a neighbor in the days following his encounter. The neighbor recounted how on the night of the incident, she'd been at a friend's house on the North Dakota side of the Red River. At several points throughout the evening, her friend's dog's behavior became erratic, including howling, running in circles, and scratching to go outside. At last the dog's owner relented, releasing the dog, who bolted into the backyard, only to come sprinting back moments later.

"My neighbor was convinced," Val says, "that whatever I saw, that dog had seen, too."

More credible, however, was the human sighting that occurred two nights later, when thirty-three-year-old Russ Johnson (no relation to Val) reported a similar sighting on a highway just outside of Vermillion, South Dakota, 430 miles due south of Marshall County.

Val was hesitant to link these events, though others, less so. Including one UFO investigator who journeyed to Val's picnic table some time later, complicating the story further by adding a third "ball of light" spotted in Beausejour, a town in the Canadian province of Manitoba, in the days leading up to Val's own encounter.

"Now if you take Beausejour and go to Vermillion and draw a straight line—well, nearly a straight line—you get to where my incident took place," Val says.

"Like . . . a corridor?"

He nods.

Later, I'll turn to Google Maps to confirm that Beausejour, Marshall County, and Vermillion do, indeed, form a near-perfect route between the ninety-fifth and ninety-sixth lines of longitude. An interesting coincidence, though I'm hardly ready to call out the National Guard. Sometimes things—even strange things—can occur without being connected. Yet Val's admission persuades me to take a closer look at the possibility of so-called UFO corridors. And I'm hardly the first to do so.

Ben Mezrich's 2016 book, *The 37th Parallel: The Secret Truth Behind America's UFO Highway*, offers a compelling case for the most well-known UFO corridor. In it, Mezrich draws attention to the disproportionate number of UFO sightings that stretch within a degree of the thirty-seventh latitudinal line, including the 1941 UFO crash in Cape Girardeau, Missouri, the 1948 Mantell UFO incident in Owensboro, Kentucky, and the 1948 UFO crash in Aztec, New Mexico, just to name a few. Adding to this strangeness are the many military institutions that also share this latitudinal line: the Pentagon, Fort Knox, and Area 51, among others.

All of which proves nothing on its own. Once again, it's a question of causality versus coincidence, and in the case of the former, trying to figure out why—of all the latitudes—the thirty-seventh is the preferred line for both our alleged interplanetary visitors and military personnel. By linking the sightings to military bases, the inference is clear: that the military is potentially involved—or perhaps responsible—for at least some of the unidentified flying objects seen in the sky. Which seems an obvious, if anticlimactic, answer. And one Tom Tulien might agree with, too.

Ask yourself: Which scenario seems most reasonable? That various extraterrestrials have set their GPS coordinates to the thirty-seventh parallel, or that the U.S. military—long known to be testing experimental aircrafts—were simply caught doing so on a few occasions?

These military aircraft, often referred to as X-planes, have long fascinated aeronautical historians. Of the many unique variations our country has had a hand in designing over the years, perhaps none are more curious than the disk-shaped, saucer-style crafts that proved of great interest to the U.S. Air Force and Army in the 1950s and early 1960s. Most notably, the Avrocar, a silver, Frisbee-like disc measuring eighteen feet in diameter and just over a meter thick. In 2012, when details of the Avrocar were at last released to the public, researchers dove deep into the treasure-trove of fascinating documents: reports, schematics, film footage, photos, and more. Upon even the most cursory glance, the Avrocar's likeness to every flying saucer ever to have graced the covers of *Fate* and *Amazing Stories* is made abundantly clear. Complete with triangular truss surrounded by a circular shell, it could easily be confused with a prop pulled from any number of 1950s-era flying saucer films. Yet the

Avrocar was more than mere prop—or was intended to be—though as aeronautical engineers soon learned, its symmetrical design, while lovely to look at, left much to be desired in the aerodynamics department.

In theory, it seemed a marvel: a versatile, vertical liftoff and landing supersonic flying machine. But in flight, it was mostly a lemon.

Despite years of effort, when the project closed in 1961, the Canadian firm hired to construct the aircraft had little to show for its efforts. Indeed, two aircraft had been built—code-named Spade and Omega—though neither managed to shoot down Soviet bombers as its designers had dreamed. The grainy film footage that remains reveals a wobbly disc that appears perpetually on the verge of crashing, a fancy-looking hovercraft, and about as useful. Which is not to discount the wildly ambitious project. After all, through its design, we learned many lessons.

Including the most obvious: it ain't easy to make a flying saucer fly.

*

Of the many mysteries surrounding the Val Johnson Incident, we can take comfort in knowing that no Avrocar was soaring through the Minnesota sky that night. Yet given what we know of the air force's experimental aircraft programs, we might wonder: Was what Val Johnson saw military in nature?

After all, just sixty miles to the southwest of Val's encounter sits Grand Forks Air Force Base, home to the 319th Air Base Wing, whose mission it is to "support 'Global Engagement' mobility operations"—an answer just vague enough to raise several more questions. Originally established in 1957 as a fighter-interceptor airbase, over the years Grand Forks Air Force Base has served several high-profile purposes, including as a home for B-52 bombers, a Sentinel anti-ballistic missile site, and, as of 1993, was placed under the purview of the Air Force Space Command.

None of this proves anything definitively regarding what crashed into Val's cruiser that night.

Sure, it's *possible* a military-designed ball of light was released from Grand Forks Air Force Base on April 27, 1979. And yes, it's *possible* that the ball of light came into direct contact with Val Johnson and his car. The problem, however, is that we have no knowledge that any ball of light has ever been created by the military, let alone any flown from that particular base at that particular time. In order for this scenario to be true, we'd have to suspend our disbelief on a number of fronts. Which an open mind allows for, of course, though the line between "open-mindedness" and "grasping at straws" can prove perilously thin.

In an effort to grasp at something, I placed a call to the Grand Forks Air Force Base, which routed me to the base historian. My question was pretty simple—*Any balls of light in the sky that night?*—though my calls were never returned.

While Val remains open to a military explanation, he's also open to a meteorological one.

"People came to me and said, 'Well, this is ball lightning from geological pressures beneath the soil. They push together and form this electrical thing, blah.' So I said, 'Fine, okay, if that's what you think it is, great. It may very well be.'"

But Val isn't ready to stake his reputation on it. And I don't blame him—particularly given the propensity with which UFO sightings are often assigned as such. (See: Project Blue Book's explanation for the Minot Air Force Base sighting.)

Yet to give this theory its due, keep in mind that Val's description for what he saw that night indeed corresponds with our general understanding of ball lightning. Though the phenomenon generally occurs in the midst of a storm, it's not unheard of to spot a blast under more stable weather conditions, such as the warm summer night in question. Moreover, the tangible evidence surrounding Val's incident is at least a little consistent with a lightning strike, most notably Val's unconsciousness, his burns, and the cracked windshield. However, what the ball lightning theory fails to explain are the fourteen lost minutes and the cruiser's bent antennas. No theories, as far as I know, can account for these particular peculiarities.

Which leaves us with what? What other possibilities might we consider?

When I press the issue with Val ("What in the world was it?"), he agrees that every possibility—including ball lightning—is worth considering. But his look sends me another message: that we shouldn't confuse possibilities with proof.

*

If there's one thing we humans love, it's stability. We like our body temperatures regulated, our blood oxygenated, and our sodium concentrations just where they ought to be. We're most comfortable when everything's in working order, and everything's in its right place. This is true of our brain as well, which takes a piece of information, encodes it, then places it in the proper filing cabinet.

However, problems arise when our brain can't find the proper cabinet, when what we know—or think we know—fails to fit anywhere. This ambiguity undermines the closure process; the result of which leads to instability and discomfort—a gnawing reminder of our inability to know our world in full.

Yet the brain, aware of our need for closure, begrudgingly obliges—hierarchizing closure over confirmation, an evolutionary tactic that has long served us well, even if it risks diluting the truth. As psychiatrist Dr. Bernard Beitman recounts, our early ancestors' ability to observe a "strange formation off in the distance" and view it as "a potential predator rather than a fallen log" surely contributed to their general safety. "Better to be safe and wrong," Beitman writes, "than to be sorry and attacked."

Given what I now know about our need for closure, I'm a bit baffled by Val's disinterest in obtaining his own. "It's just a strange occurrence that happened to me," he shrugs. "Every day people are having strange occurrences for whatever reason. I just happened to be the target on that particular evening."

"You don't need more closure than that?"

"I'm fine with it."

And I'm skeptical. Not of Val's ability to have made peace with his mystery, but of my own ability to do so. I can't help but winnow down explanations to fulfill my own need for closure. Yet when closure remains elusive, we're forced to turn to patterns instead—anything to help us find the proper file.

"Pattern pleases us, rewards a mind seduced and yet exhausted by complexity," Diane Ackerman writes in a 2004 essay for the *New York Times*. "We crave pattern, and find it all around us, in petals, sand dunes, pine cones, contrails." These patterns, Ackerman argues, "reassure us that life is orderly."

"The brain is a pattern-mad supposing machine," Ackerman continues. "Given just a little stimuli, it divines the probable. When information abounds, it recognizes familiar patterns and acts with conviction."

And here's the kicker: "If there's not much for the senses to report, the brain imagines the rest."

It seems the ultimate betrayal: our minds outsmarting our sense of reason. It's a claim that threatens to undermine much of what we think we know, calling into question our powers of observation, not to mention our credibility as well-intentioned witnesses of our world.

Thirty-eight years after his incident, Val seems to have persuaded his brain to knock it off with its imaginings. He saw what he saw—end of story. Though that wasn't always the case.

In the fall of 1979—mere months after the incident—Val signed up for EMT courses in Grafton, North Dakota, just a short drive from his home in Oslo. One night while driving to class he was suddenly overcome with an unexplainably strong compulsion for lemon drops.

"I'm sorry . . . lemon drops?" I ask, interrupting Val's story. "Like . . . the candy?"

Of the many strange things I've heard today, somehow this seems the strangest.

"Stay with me now," Val says. "Now, my instructor was a psychology fellow from the University of North Dakota, so I talked to him about it at break time."

The instructor listened carefully to Val's unexplainable lemon drop craving and agreed to do a bit of research. A week later, during a class break, the professor took Val aside and said, "Tell me what a lemon drop looks like."

Perplexed, Val played along, describing a lemon drop as an "oblong shape with a line down the middle."

The instructor—who had knowledge of Val's incident—said: "I think you saw something like that. Something oval-shaped with a defining margin through the middle."

The instructor continued: "Your eyes saw this, and your brain experienced this, and the brain does not know how to classify it. It absolutely has to put it in an envelope someplace. And the nearest thing your brain can come up with is lemon drops."

"So your brain needed a way to account for what you saw," I say.

Val nods. "It had to put it in an envelope," he says.

*

When trying to put Val's story in an envelope, I return to the tangible: the damage inflicted upon Val's 1977 Ford LTD. It's the one part of the story that always makes sense, or mostly makes sense, at least.

In the aftermath of the incident, investigators noted various points of damage, including the aforementioned broken headlight, the bent antennas, the quarter-sized dent in the hood. And we can't forget the broken plastic on the hazard light or the cracked windshield either. All of this damage occurred in a direct line, indicating that whatever struck the car did so in a fashion quite similar to a projectile. Yet despite the object's power, it also managed quite a bit of finesse—cracking the glass without shattering it, bending the antennas without scraping off the bugs. The seemingly precise pressures that acted upon the car made for yet another head-scratcher, one more mystery to add to the others.

And then, of course, there's the mystery of the glass from the broken headlight.

"The glass from the headlight was laying on the highway, on a puddle, or an area about this big around," Val tells me, making a plate-sized circle with his hands. "Now if I'm doing sixty miles an hour you'd think there'd be a *trail* of glass, but all the glass is right there."

Which, according to physics, leads us to believe that the vehicle was stationary at the time of the glass shattering. But it wasn't. While the car was indeed stopped shortly after the impact, Val has no memory of placing his foot on the brakes. All he knows for certain was that when he woke approximately thirty-nine minutes later, the car was blocking both lanes of the road, the keys were still in the ignition, and the engine was dead.

The damage to the car remains the best physical evidence we've got. Val's injuries healed, but the car has faithfully preserved each nick and dent. Today, the car resides in a showroom at the Marshall County Museum, where it holds the distinction of being the most visited exhibition in town. Not to mention the most famous 1977 Ford LTD Marshall County has ever known.

*

Of the many theories of what happened to Val Johnson, there's at least one we've yet to address: that Val perpetuated a hoax.

Though the veracity of Val's story was confirmed by both the sheriff's department and the Center for UFO Studies, there was at least one man who questioned the events that did—or did not—transpire that fateful night.

Phillip Klass—dubbed the "Sherlock Holmes of UFOlogy"—dedicated much of his life to debunking UFO sightings. Though it didn't win him any popularity contests within the UFO community, it was indeed important work—a check and balance for the more overzealous believers. From the late 1960s to the early 2000s, he'd become embroiled in a number of public disagreements with fellow researchers, earning a reputation that garnered him, as one fellow debunker put it, both "grateful followers" and "legions of detractors." Klass was quite comfortable in his role as contrarian. He viewed it as a public service of sorts, a full-throated voice of skepticism within a community that, to his mind, was often a little too quick to believe.

Though he was dismissive of the title "debunker," it was well earned. As Klass offered one counter theory after another (attributing sightings to plasma, ball lightning, hoaxes, human error, etc.), some UFOlogists grumbled that nothing could ever persuade a man so hell-bent on disbelieving. Not so, rebutted Klass, who in a 1999 interview claimed it was his "fondest hope" that a UFO would land on his patio and abduct him. (Admittedly, it's hard to gauge the sincerity of his claim given that a few lines later he noted the large royalty checks he imagined might accompany such an encounter.)

Despite all his feather-ruffling, even Klass's detractors conceded that his work contributed meaningfully to UFO studies. And to his credit, Klass himself agreed that "roughly 97, 98 percent of the people who report seeing UFOs are fundamentally intelligent, honest people who have seen something . . . that they cannot explain."

By all accounts, Val Johnson fits snugly within this camp—intelligent, honest, and admittedly baffled. Yet Klass was less certain of Val's intentions, his investigation into the sighting leading him to two possible conclusions.

The first—offered with extreme cheekiness—describes a version of events in which Val was attacked by "malicious UFOnauts" who proceeded to take a "hammer-like device" to the car and then "reached inside . . . to set back the hands of the watch on Johnson's arm and the clock on the car's dashboard."

And the second: "Or, the incident is a hoax."

When I press Val on Klass's assessment, he shrugs it off.

"Fine. Have at it," he chuckles. "When [Klass] contacts me and wants to buy my line of vitamins and supplements, then we'll talk."

Whether it was extraterrestrial, military, or meteorological—who can say for sure?

Not Val. And not me either.

"You know, you've got a great mystery on your hands," I tell Val as I take my final sip of coffee. "But what you've confirmed for me is that maybe we don't need an answer for every mystery in our world. The mystery makes it fun."

"Mystery," Val says, reaching for his cinnamon roll, "is the jelly on top of the toast of our otherwise normal and uninteresting lives."

I chuckle.

"It's the icing on our cinnamon roll," I agree.

Part 3

THE WEIRD

The Universe is under no obligation
to make sense to you.

NEIL DEGRASSE TYSON

CASE FILE #7

The Hodag

1893–Present

NAME: THE HODAG

SCIENTIFIC NAME: DEFIES CLASSIFICATION

LOCATION: RHINELANDER, WISCONSIN

DESCRIPTION: APPROXIMATELY 185 POUNDS AND SEVEN FEET LONG; A CROSS BETWEEN A LIZARD AND AN OX COMPLETE WITH RAZOR-SHARP FANGS AND HORNS. THE CREATURE IS SAID TO HAVE GLOWING GREEN EYES AND SMOKE CURLING FROM HIS NOSTRILS. EARLY VERSIONS OF THE HODAG DESCRIBED THE BEAST AS BLACK; LATER, HIS COLOR CHANGED TO A FRIENDLIER GREEN.

WITNESS TESTIMONY: "THIS IS NOT A WOOD CARVING WE ARE TALKING ABOUT, BUT A BEAST WITH THE POWER TO RIP THE BELLY OUT OF THE BIGGEST BEAR, NEEDLE-SHARP HORNS ON THE END OF HIS TAIL, GLOWING GREEN EYES AND FLARING RED NOSTRILS AND A SMELL THAT WOULD DRIVE A SKUNK OFF A GUT PILE, REMEMBER? THOSE EYES AND NOSTRILS WOULD SEND THE BIGGEST, MEANEST LUMBERJACK RUNNING FOR HIS MOMMY, LONG BEFORE THE HORNS, CLAWS, AND TAIL POINTS WOULD COME INTO PLAY." JERRY SHIDELL, 2017

CONCLUSION: THE LEGEND LIVES. THE CREATURE . . . NOT SO MUCH.

We have come to see the Hodag and we won't be turned away.

"Come on," my five-year-old son calls to me, "hurry up or we'll miss it."

How do I tell him that we can't miss it? That it's impossible to miss something that doesn't even exist? Nonetheless, I quicken my pace

Fig. 11. Gene Shepard and local citizenry point their pitchforks at the Hodag in Rhinelander, Wisconsin, around 1899. Courtesy of the Wisconsin Historical Society—WHi-36382.

("I'm coming, I'm coming"), weaving through dozens of other Oneida County fairgoers in an effort to catch a glimpse of the most horrible creature the region's ever known.

Welcome to Rhinelander, Wisconsin—home of the Hodag. The town makes no secret of their monster; in fact, they've embraced it fully, as evidenced by the enormous Hodag statue displayed just outside the chamber of commerce.

But we've journeyed here today, not for any statue, but for the "real thing." Or as real as a fake thing can be.

Just ahead of us on the makeshift stage, Jerry Shidell (playing the part of nineteenth-century Hodag originator Gene Shepard) works the crowd with his huckster's charm.

"Step right up, folks! In eight and a half minutes the Hodag show will begin. That's right! In eight and a half minutes you will see a real, live Hodag!"

"Like . . . the actual monster?" my son asks, wide-eyed.

"I mean, that's what the guy says . . ." I shrug.

Jerry (or should I say Gene?) smiles as the other children in the crowd begin asking similar questions of their own parents—*How big is it? How bad is it? Is it hungry?* Jerry returns his attention to his partner, Junior, who straightens his lumberjack hat as he prepares for the role of a lifetime: introducing fairgoers to the Hodag itself.

Mythic as he is mysterious, dangerous as he is discrete, the Hodag (allegedly) sits tethered just behind a curtain within the tent.

Eight and a half minutes later, we anxiously await the show to begin.

"You ready?" Jerry whispers.

Junior nods.

"Then here goes nothing . . ."

A cleared throat, followed by: "Greetings! Now then, who's here to see the Hodag?"

We in the crowd surge forward, anxious for a spot inside the tent. The stale air mixes with the heat, producing a distinctly human smell: not quite body odor but close, the olfactory equivalent of anticipation, perhaps, or the pungency of fear.

"Surely by now most of you know the Hodag story," Jerry begins, and though we do, he takes advantage of his captive audience to tell it again. We stand at rapt attention as he recounts every detail of the harrowing story—the hunt, its capture, as well as Gene Shepard's heroic role in taming the beast.

"And now, without further ado," Jerry concludes, his voice turning to a whisper, "Junior and I look forward to introducing you to . . . the antediluvian creature itself!"

Jerry gives Junior the nod, signaling his young assistant to move behind the white screen and reach for the bungee-cord leash (allegedly) attached to the Hodag.

Junior gives it a pull, and the beast's silhouette pulls back.

We chuckle as Junior's launched forward, struggling to stay on his feet.

"Try it again," Jerry coaxes, though when Junior does, he's met with a warning growl, prompting him to drop the leash and run for cover.

"Oh, come on now," Jerry prods, "give the people what they want, Junior! And they want to see the Hodag. Am I right, folks?"

"Yeah!" we holler. "Show us the Hodag! Come on, Junior!"

At our coaxing, Junior takes one last crack at pulling the Hodag into view, stepping behind the screen once more to fight the silhouette.

Another growl, and then, chaos: hollers and screams and a cloud of chicken feathers wafting through the air.

"Shepard, I need some help!" Junior cries, his face momentarily visible over the lip of the screen. "I need . . ."

Suddenly a razor-sharp claw reaches above the screen, pulling Junior back down while their silhouettes offer a dramatic, visual play-by-play.

We watch in jaw-dropped horror as Junior at last escapes from the Hodag's clutches, hurling himself back in front of the screen, his shirt in tatters.

Jerry scratches his head before offering his preplanned apology.

"Well I'm sorry folks, but . . . we're just not going to be able to show him today. It's very unsafe for us to bring him out. Again, I'm sorry. The exit's to your left."

"Aw, man!" my son says. "We didn't even get to see him!"

Grumbling, we all make our way toward the tent flap as Jerry and Junior share the briefest of smiles.

"I guess that means we'll have to come back next year," I say.

Which, of course, is exactly the point.

*

One hundred twenty-four years after its "discovery," the Hodag remains as alive and well as ever. By which I mean: not alive and well at all. But at least its story remains alive and well, and some of the credit goes to sixty-nine-year-old actor, entrepreneur, and former Rhinelander mayor Jerry Shidell, who, year after year, faithfully plays Gene Shepard in the Oneida County Fair reenactments. Though the original Hodag story will always belong to Shepard, who in addition to being a successful timber cruiser, was a bit of an actor and entrepreneur himself.

As the story goes, one October afternoon in 1893, thirty-nine-year-old Gene Shepard was strolling among the pine and hemlock trees when he stumbled upon an unknown creature skulking in the woods near Rhinelander. He could hardly believe his eyes: the black beast resembled a cross between a lizard and an ox, complete with razor-sharp fangs and horns, not to mention the fire and smoke smoldering from his nostrils. The creature weighed in at 185 pounds and was about seven feet long. Shepard froze at the mere sight of it, his eyes drifting across its spiky back as the creature's glowing green eyes stared back at him. As horrible as it was to view, it was equally horrible to smell, its stench described by Shepard as "a combination of buzzard meat and skunk perfume."

Startled, Shepard made his retreat into town, where he rallied the finest hunters, returning to the location to take the beast dead or alive. Upon their approach, the hunting dogs were soon torn to shreds, at which point the hunters opened fire to little avail. Desperate, they turned to their dynamite sticks, hurling them at the creature, who absorbed the blasts until catching fire and smoldering to death—but only after nine horrific hours of thrashing.

Or so one version of the story goes.

There are plenty of others, all of which serve as fine contributions to late nineteenth- and early twentieth-century lumber camp lore. But the Hodag—much like Paul Bunyan—managed to extend beyond the confines of the bunkhouses, reaching into the world of popular culture as well. Stories were big business, or had the potential to be, and in 1896, when Gene Shepard learned that Rhinelander's Oneida County Fair had no major draw, he took it upon himself to rectify the situation. He'd already concocted the Hodag story a few years prior; now, all he needed was the Hodag itself.

Retreating to his barn, Shepard began carving a creature befitting his tale.

I can't help but envision this moment as the North Woods' equivalent of *Frankenstein*: the mad-with-power Shepard cobbling his creature to life as lightning blazes overhead. Reaching for his tools, he carves fangs, inserts horns, and tests the sharpness of each spike with his fingertips.

Once he'd carved the beast, Shepard needed only to revise his tale, offering a version that didn't end with the Hodag burned to ash as he'd previously recounted. He was more than up to the task. In the days leading up to the fair, Shepard publicized his revised version of the Hodag's "capture" by way of a front page article in the local newspaper.

In this version, a group of lumbermen were wandering the banks near Lake Creek when they came upon the Hodag holed up in his den. Well aware that the creature could never be overpowered by strength alone, they relied on their wits instead. Dousing a cloth in chloroform, they slid it onto the end of a long stick and pushed it within sniffing range of the Hodag's snout. The chloroform did its work, downing the beast long enough for the men to restrain it. At which point the lumbermen did the logical thing: placed it in a wagon, transported it to Rhinelander, then housed it in a pit for safekeeping.

In the opening days of the fair, Shepard welcomed visitors into a tent to catch a glimpse of the beast. And, indeed, a glimpse was all he offered them. Mindful that the mystery is often better than the reveal, Shepard did his part to create the conditions to ensure that his Hodag remained conveniently out of sight. He held onlookers to a safe distance, kept the lights low, and allowed visitors only the briefest, neck-craning peek.

"To further convince the spectators," writes Hodag scholar Kurt Kortenhof, "Shepard's sons manipulated the bogus animal through a system of hidden wires."

One of those sons was Layton Shepard, who for years continued to play a supporting role in his father's ruse.

"[Dad] was just an expert of leading these people into a certain state and then scaring them half to death," Layton recalled years later.

It didn't hurt that the people of Rhinelander *wanted* to believe—at least in the beginning. After all, what town doesn't want to be home to a monster? Or anything, for that matter, that had the power to make it unique?

*

In March 2017—121 years after Shepard's infamous chloroform-inspired capture of the Hodag—I make my first solo trip into Rhinelander, barely entering the city limits before coming face-to-face with the ferocious beast himself.

The gigantic Hodag statue greets me from his place outside the chamber of commerce, his fanged grin all but impossible to miss while heading east on U.S. 8. I'd seen photos, but none had done him justice. What stands before me is a red-eyed sentinel, his right paw extended into the air as if daring any out-of-town doubters to challenge his existence. Of course, such an ostentatious creature has often proved a ripe target for vandals, and since 2012, the Hodag has endured a couple of lost claws, as well as an unsolicited spray painting. Nevertheless, the fiber glass wonder persists. And his presence serves as the perfect welcome to Rhinelander: not exactly a red carpet, but a toothy, horned grimace instead.

Like any good tourist, I stop for my photo, and while there, step inside the chamber of commerce where I strike up a conversation with a pair of employees, both of whom are more than happy to speak on the Hodag's behalf.

"No matter what day, there's someone out there," the first woman tells me, nodding to the statue just beyond the window. "It could be bad weather, good weather, weekends, there's always someone."

Since both women have spent their entire lives in Rhinelander, I ask the obvious question: Is it weird having a monster for the town mascot?

"It was never weird having the Hodag," says the second woman. "It was always just . . . the Hodag."

"It was a matter of fact," the first woman agrees.

What was? The creature's existence, or its story?

Both women are quick to confirm that the Hodag is merely a story. And yet, there's nothing "mere" about that. Though a living, breathing Hodag never roamed the woods around Rhinelander, that minor detail hardly kept the creature from gaining national notoriety.

They direct my eyes toward the wall behind them, upon which hangs an animation frame from a 2012 episode of *Scooby-Doo! Mystery, Inc.*

"Did you know we made *Scooby-Doo?*" the first woman asks, nodding to the Hodag drawing featured within the frame.

"I did." I smile. "My son and I stumbled upon that episode just a few months back."

"Well did you know we made J. K. Rowling's *Fantastic Beasts?*" asks the second woman.

This is news to me.

I soon learn that Rowling's updated edition of her book features six new creatures, three of which come from lumberjack lore—the Hidebehind, the Wampus Cat, and, of course, the Hodag. A part of me is astonished that a folk creature from Rhinelander, Wisconsin, found its way into J. K. Rowling's book, though perhaps I shouldn't be.

Stories travel, after all. And as they do, they change.

*

Once upon a time, Rhinelander was a lumber town, and then one day, it wasn't. Though lumber was what initially drew the strong-backed, axe-wielding men to the region, once the jack pine and Norway pine ran out, so, too, did that way of life. Yet in the beginning, town founders had every reason to be hopeful. Rhinelander had a railroad, a natural resource, and the men to help bring that resource to market. And for timber cruisers like Gene Shepard, there was plenty of money to be made. Though the town originally consisted of little more than a tent camp, by 1884 its population blossomed to fifteen hundred. Within six years, it would boast a total of eight sawmills, solidifying Rhinelander as a lumber town. At least for a little while.

Today, it's a different place. With a population hovering around seventy-six hundred, the city's main industry now centers around the paper mill, which employs between four hundred and five hundred local residents. The city's forests and lakes also contribute to Rhinelander's recreational economy, though as many locals tell me, it's the mill that keeps the place afloat. As powerful as the Hodag is, not even his allure (and the

Fig. 12. Jerry Shidell playing the part of Hodag creator Gene Shepard at the 2017 Oneida County Fair in Rhinelander, Wisconsin. Courtesy of the author.

tourism dollars that accompany him) would be enough to make up for the lost jobs were the mill to go away. If it came to that, the city would be forced to find a new way forward, much as it did at the turn of the twentieth century when the trees ran out and the Hodag rose to prominence.

Few folks know Rhinelander's story better than Jerry Shidell. I'd arranged to interview him a week prior, during a phone conversation in which I asked if there were any "Gene-Shepard-specific places" where we might meet.

"Well," Jerry replied, "I live next door to the barn where Shepard used to keep his Hodag. Think that might work?"

I agreed that it might.

As I pull into Jerry's driveway days later, my eyes drift to the three-story stone barn directly to my right. And beyond that, Gene Shepard's studio, as well as his once beautiful home.

The car's barely in park before a boisterous Jerry greets me at his door. "Welcome," he calls, "come on in."

Within moments we're seated across from one another in his study, the wood stove crackling just a few feet away.

"When you bought this property, did you know its historical Hodag significance?" I ask, nodding toward Shepard's former home.

Jerry assures me he didn't. In fact, when he and his wife arrived in Rhinelander in 1974, they'd barely even heard of the Hodag.

"But when you're here for a while, it just becomes something people talk about," he shrugs. "You see a sign and you begin to read about it. But it really started to gel when I was mayor between 1978 and 1980," he says. "As mayor, you really have to embrace it."

Which he did, and continues to, most notably by playing the role of Gene Shepard at every opportunity.

"How does one prepare for the role of Gene Shepard?" I ask.

"Well," he begins, "if you really wanted to be Gene Shepard you'd have to become a drunkard, because he was a bit of a drinker, a practical joker, a *very* big practical joker, a womanizer, and a braggart. Any one of those will get you to Gene Shepard," he chuckles, "but none of those will ingratiate you with the audience."

I'm surprised by his candor. Shepard, after all, is nearly Rhinelander royalty. At least according to some. Though to others, he's the mountebank of the North Woods, a snake oil salesman who, rather than hawking his wares, hawked a monster instead.

It's just one of the ironies of the Gene Shepard story: though he was one of the most successful timber cruisers in the region—a man who wandered Wisconsin's unexplored wilderness and came out with clear maps and lumbering tracts—he's hardly remembered for that. Nor is he remembered for his timber cruising beyond the region—explorations as far flung as Canada and the West Coast.

"He's lived on because he created one critter unique to the world," Jerry says, "and we've adopted it as our own."

By the late 1800s, Shepard had become so proficient at his Hodag shows that he moved beyond the county fair circuit to offer more personalized glimpses in his barn. Passersby traveling through Rhinelander would often take a moment to knock on Shepard's door in the hopes of a catching a glimpse.

Shepard would generally oblige, using a signal phrase ("Boys, make sure the Hodag is tied up so he doesn't get loose!") to prepare his sons, Layton and Claude, for the task of hiding in hay bales and using wires to shock the creature into motion.

Shepard always kept the curiosity seekers at the edge of the barn as he entered to check on the creature's temperament, at which point the snarls and growls would reverberate throughout the structure, prompting a breathless Shepard to run back to safety, emerging from the dark in a shredded suit—not unlike Junior's.

"But he wasn't dumb enough to rip a new suit every time," Jerry explains. "He just had an old torn suit in there. He would just change his shirt."

In his newly disheveled state, Shepard would then use the same excuse Jerry co-opted years later, disappointedly informing the anxious viewers that there would be no show today, that it was simply too dangerous to risk pulling the Hodag from his hole.

"And all that happened here?" I ask, turning toward the barn next door.

"You bet," Jerry agrees. "Come on, I'll give you the tour."

Jerry leads me outside, pausing before Shepard's barn, a giant, three-story structure which—in addition to the pit—was another so-called holding pen for the Hodag.

"This whole area was called The Pines," Jerry says, pointing to Shepard's former compound—the house, the study, the barn. "He had tunnels that connected all of them. But here's the weird thing about the tunnels, and nobody's ever been able to figure it out. Here's a guy who could go out into the woods and timber cruise for days at a time, weeks at a time, but he didn't want to go outside to go to his barn or his den."

Indeed, it's a hard circle to square, but fitting, too, for an enigmatic man like Shepard.

Jerry repeats the story he'd told me previously: how out-of-towners would leave the train station and hustle over to this very barn to catch a glimpse of the Hodag, even though they always left disappointed.

Jerry and I leave the barn and head down a path leading toward the Pelican River. Along the way we stop near a hole in the ground, which Jerry informs me is the Hodag's former home.

"Here's the pit," he says, pointing to the hole. "It's filled in over the years. It was deeper before."

Confused, I ask: "So Shepard told visitors that he kept the Hodag in this pit, but really he kept it in the barn?"

"Well, the story, I suspect, evolved over time."

There's no question about it. Over time this story has been spun more times than a top, every rendition adding to or subtracting from the original tale. For hardened historians, such disparate versions must seem maddening, but for others, like me, every variation adds vibrancy to the original, forever ensuring that the story remains fresh.

As we leave the pit, Jerry points me toward Shepard Park directly off to our right.

"The Shepard family donated the land to the city," Jerry says, "and originally designated it to be used as a park. But after a while the restrictions came off, which is why we have the old water treatment plant on it now," he says, pointing me toward the now abandoned facility.

"It's kind of ironic," I say, "that the guy who made a reputation by dealing in bull crap now has a waste treatment plant on the park that bears his name."

"I never thought about that!" Jerry chuckles. "But you know, that's a good one!"

*

Back inside near the wood stove, I ask Jerry the same question I'd asked at the chamber of commerce: Did people ever actually believe in the Hodag?

"Oh, there's no question that people believed in the Hodag when Shepard first developed it," Jerry says, "at least the people who came to the fairgrounds, the carnival. Back then people were a little more susceptible to beliefs, and especially since we didn't have the instant answers we have today, the ability to prove or disprove almost anything within the hour. There was much less communication," he continues, "much less knowledge of the whole world being mapped out, so to speak. You've got a wild wilderness out there, hundreds of thousands of acres of wildness, and who knows, very easily something could have developed out there."

Rhinelander's remoteness, coupled with limited information, a showman of Shepard's caliber, and a town in need of a new industry, all converged to create the perfect conditions to spin a yarn of Hodag proportions.

And it's been quite good for the town.

"The Hodag makes us a place on the map," Jerry says, echoing an answer eerily familiar to the one Miles Wilson had offered related to Oscar's impact on Churubusco, Indiana. "It gives us a unique mascot that nobody else has and nobody else will ever get."

"Some communities are hesitant to embrace such a strange thing," I say. "But there seems to be real benefit for communities who take advantage of it, at least in terms of tourism. During your time as mayor, did you find it made more sense to embrace the strange rather than write it off?"

"It's strange," Jerry concedes, "but you know, people like strange."

For proof, you need only take a walk through downtown Rhinelander, where the Hodag's image is always within view: on a poster, or a sticker, or a storefront.

Today, over fifty local businesses have co-opted the Hodag in some fashion. One can get his oil changed at Hodag Express Lube, then purchase a firearm at Hodag Gun & Loan, then complete the day by enjoying a bit of "Hodag Poop" from the local candy store. The Hodag's ubiquity is proof of its lasting power, and today, locals know to cash in.

But it's only over the last decade or so that Jerry's been able to fully understand the power of Rhinelander's beast. After logging over 140,000 miles of road tripping with his wife throughout the continental U.S., Jerry often returns home with a deeper appreciation for what they have in their own backyard.

"We've gone to a lot of towns, and they're nice little towns, nice little places, but I would guess that the thing that's missing is a rallying point. Something to identify with. Yes, we have a nice area here—trees, lakes, away from the big crowds—but we're not the only one that has that. There are a thousand other cities that are in unique places and we've been to a lot of them."

Jerry tells me about the vistas of the west, the oceans down south, the mountains they've enjoyed while traveling east. But in all of those places, he's struggled to see what brings those towns together.

"Don't get me wrong, we have our warts, we have our problems. Every city does. But," Jerry says, "we also have something unique."

"You'll always have the Hodag," I say. "Except, of course, that nobody really has the Hodag."

Jerry laughs.

Now I'm catching on.

*

It's difficult to walk the fine line between the truth and the trick: a fact I'm reminded of just days after my time in Rhinelander.

Despite all I've learned about Gene Shepard, it's all come secondhand. What I need is to hear from someone who knew Shepard personally, though since his acquaintances have all since passed, I turn to a 1963 interview with Layton Shepard, Gene's youngest son, who often provided the growls and shocks to bring his father's story to life. Though Gene Shepard receives the bulk of the credit for the Hodag hoax, Layton gained a bit of notoriety for posing as the downed child on the forest floor in the now famous 1899 photo. In it, the seven-year-old Layton tries to protect himself with his half-raised arm while the ferocious beast peers down at him like a disgruntled stegosaurus. Layton and his attacker are flanked by over a dozen well-armed men, creating a highly sensationalized photo that, for years to come, served as photographic "proof" (albeit, not very convincing) of the Hodag's existence.

Speaking of the Hodag years later, Layton refused to sugarcoat the creature's adverse side effects: "To be quite frank," he said, "the 'Hodag' was quite a painful thing to the family."

Painful in that it served as a continual diversion from Shepard's duties as a husband and father. Surely he was aware of the personal price he paid by perpetuating his hoax, yet it seemed he paid it willingly.

"You couldn't call [the Hodag] a mixed blessing," Layton remarked more than half a century later, "because there was very little blessing connected with it. He manufactured the thing. He had the country fooled on it."

And "fooling the country" had always been his intent, at least in part. Shepard was convinced that the best way to boost the town was by giving outsiders a reason to visit. Upon viewing Rhinelander's natural splendor for themselves, Shepard believed out-of-towners might put down roots, invest bullishly, and help the town thrive and prosper. The Hodag was simply the impetus to get them there.

"By no means is all the progress to be credited to the Hodag," Shepard wrote later in life, "but the Hodag did his bit! Not only hundreds, but thousands of people came to view the Hodag . . . and not one of them went away without having learned a little more about north Wisconsin."

Layton, however, questioned his father's civic-minded intentions.

"All of the things that he thought up were done for the purpose of attracting attention to the name, Shepard," he remarked.

Indeed, Gene Shepard's legacy has persisted locally, though for many, his personal story remains as mysterious as the Hodag. Both are rooted in the same strange history, and what we know of them we know mostly as a result of the stories told about them.

"That's the way folklore develops," folklorist L. G. Sorden told Layton during their 1963 interview. "Somebody starts a story, and the first story may be absolutely credulous, and then they add to it, and so on."

It's a phenomenon I've witnessed throughout this project: a wonder of storytelling, but a complication, too. How a character can quickly become larger than life, though not without a few growing pains. Just ask Gene Shepard, who became ensnared in his own yarn, his creation consuming his legacy.

To understand Gene Shepard, I'm left to rely upon his son's complex assessment. Layton Shepard, who in one breath tells us his father was a madman, and in the next, tells us he was a genius, too. Throughout the interview, Layton grapples with similarly contradictory views of his father, eventually conceding that his father was "a man with two personalities."

Yet even within Layton's less-than-glowing assessment of his father, he offered hints of admiration.

"I never saw a man like him," Layton said, recounting how his father could lift a ten-foot boat from the water as if it was nothing, how he shot from the hip with near perfect accuracy, and how he built a cabin with little more than "an ax and a couple of days." These descriptions harken back to another larger-than-life figure, Paul Bunyan, who Shepard helped shape by way of his own retellings in the North Woods' bunkhouses and beyond.

While much is known of Shepard's knack for spinning bunkhouse yarns, far less is known about his ability—or willingness—to tell the occasional bedtime story to his sons. Growing up, Layton remembered his father being gone for weeks—a sacrifice made by many timber cruisers whose livelihoods depended upon their ability to venture deep into unexplored terrain.

While most timber cruisers were accompanied by a partner, Layton remembered his father working mostly alone, adding that nobody worked with him "for any length of time." Even upon his returns to civilization, Shepard struggled to keep hired help around the house. "He was just too ornery," Layton said.

Though much has been said of Shepard's public persona, it's his private moments in the Wisconsin wilderness that remain most intriguing. Who was Shepard when there was no audience to perform for? What did he do for weeks on end as he surveyed the land, drew the maps, and speculated the virgin timber? Did he practice his stories round the campfire even when there was no one to hear? And if so, at what point did he dream up his Hodag?

Between the ages of ten and twelve, Layton eased his father's isolation by occasionally accompanying him into the wilderness, weaving through the tamarack swamps in search of valuable land. Layton worked the chain, assisting in the surveying process as best he could. It was dreadful work, Layton remembered, especially due to the mosquitoes that clouded the air so thickly that he could "hardly see the chain."

Though Layton swatted them away as best he could, his father refused even to acknowledge such a minor annoyance.

"He would have them thick on the back of his neck and wouldn't even raise his hands," Layton remarked.

Despite his labor, Layton noted that his father "never made a dime on anything."

But in fact, for a time, Shepard made quite a living, though his efforts at diversifying—cutting lumber rather than surveying it, overseeing a resort, etc.—proved less than profitable. Had he simply bought timber rather than speculated for others, Layton believes his father might've amassed incredible wealth.

"My dad was his own worst enemy," Layton said. "He could have been one of the wealthiest men in the state of Wisconsin had he tried. But, he always had to try something different."

Yet for a young man with limited education who struck out on his own at fourteen, he didn't do half bad financially. The problem, however, was that for all Shepard's skill at making money, he was just as good at spending it. He bought race horses, houses, even financed a boat so big it couldn't properly float down the Wisconsin River. This latter example serves as a perfect metaphor for Shepard himself. Here was a man who dreamed too big for his own good, and as a result, often overlooked the little things that mattered.

This was certainly true in his personal life, where Shepard struggled to be a decent father and husband. Late in life he divorced, remarried ("in the midst of a drunken stupor" one report claimed), became estranged from his children, and—after a series of lawsuits and near bankruptcies—tragically died alone in his home on West Prospect Street.

A sworn affidavit from Mildred Shepard, his wife for over thirty years, noted that her ex-husband "repeatedly laid violent hands on her, choked her, abused her and threw cold water on her, repeatedly calling her vile names and otherwise misused her without cause or excuse."

After reading Layton's acknowledgments of his father's dual personalities, I think of the Hodag, who himself came in two varieties. Initially, the Hodag was the all-black "antediluvian monster of the North," a creature pulled straight from the bowels of hell. But later, he became a tourist-friendly critter: a sleepy-eyed grin forever spread across his furry green face. That Shepard possessed attributes of both versions of his beast seems fitting. Unquestionably he was a friend to the burgeoning community, though a foe, too, to many of the people who inhabited it.

From his practical jokes to his alcohol-inspired antics (Shepard was once discovered naked and asleep in a downtown storefront), Hodag scholar Kurt Kortenhof notes that Shepard "eventually found himself alienated from both his family and, toward the end of his life, from society in general."

Surely it was a bitter pill: realizing that the town he'd helped create had turned its back on him. By the end of his life, the boisterous, bunkhouse tale-teller appeared to have vanished, leaving behind a man with a diminished tale and no one left to listen.

As for the wood-carved Hodag, it's believed to have met its own tragic end in a fire alongside Ballard Lake, home to a cabin-turned-resort which Shepard cheekily named "The House of the Good Shepard." Shepard's time as a resort proprietor was short lived, and following its one and only season in existence, he sold the property and moved on to better investments.

Unsurprisingly, the details surrounding the Hodag's demise remain murky. Was the wood-carved creature simply a casualty of a house fire as many have claimed? Or, in the version I've dreamed up, did Shepard—perhaps in a bout of sadness for his personal failures perpetuated by the beast—pile kindling beneath his Hodag and light the match himself?

The lack of closure seems a fitting end to a story so hard to pin down. There are simply too many knots to untangle, many of which Kortenhof enumerates: size, color, diet, and even the number of Hodags allegedly "captured." Which is to say the Hodag story remains in constant flux. As do most stories that endure the effects of time, distance, and a lack of a confirmable written record. But arguably, it's the variation that keeps listeners listening.

What new detail might emerge this time around? they wonder. *What new flourish might add to the myth?*

*

A few days removed from my visit with Jerry Shidell, I, too, add to the myth—stumbling upon a startling fact in the transcribed pages of Layton Shepard's interview.

According to Layton, the Hodag never "lived" in the barn alongside Jerry's house; in fact, it was likely never anywhere near that property. The Hodag was created and shown at the family's Pelham Street house just a few miles away, where the Shepards lived until 1906. They didn't move into their new home alongside Jerry's future home until later, long after the Hodag burned near Ballard Lake.

I fear the truth might prove devastating to Jerry, who for years has recounted the version of the story that he believed to be true. And it was a story that certainly seemed true to most listeners. Though I had my own questions related to timeline, I likely wouldn't have investigated further had Layton Shepard not confirmed my suspicion. But he did, in no uncertain terms.

When asked if the Hodag was ever at The Pines (the property alongside Jerry's), Layton replied with a simple, "No."

Okay, I rationalize, *but maybe there was a second Hodag that later resided there?*

This theory, too, is shot down when Layton confirms that there was only ever one. While the legend expanded to include the capture of a female Hodag, as well as the "discovery" of thirteen or so Hodag eggs, Shepard never appeared to have employed his woodcarving skills to back up his tales with additional physical proof.

I share the news with Jerry in the most cowardly way imaginable: via email.

Jerry writes back within hours, and in his reply, reprises his role as Gene Shepard.

"Ah, an interesting tidbit," Jerry agrees. "But, remember, he is talking about a wood carving. I'm talking the real thing, in the basement, snarling, growling, ripping things to shreds, including my brand new suit."

I smile at the mention of "my."

"This is not a wood carving we are talking about," he continues, "but a beast with the power to rip the belly out of the biggest bear, needle-sharp horns on the end of his tail, glowing green eyes and flaring red nostrils and a smell that would drive a skunk off a gut pile, remember? Those eyes and nostrils would send the biggest, meanest lumberjack running for his mommy, long before the horns, claws, and tail points would come into play."

Jerry concludes his defense better than I could've imagined:

"You can keep your wood carving on S. Pelham St., the civilized part of town, but for me the real thing is in the barn in the pines, in the wild."

I shut my laptop, certain that he's right.

When facts fall short, the fiction flourishes.

And when dealing with a creature that lives and dies at the mercy of our memory, how can any interpretation ever be wrong?

CASE FILE #8

Project ELF

1968–2004

NAME: PROJECT ELF. (EARLIER VERSIONS OF THE PROJECT WERE CALLED PROJECT SANGUINE AND PROJECT SEAFARER.)

SCIENTIFIC NAME: N/A

LOCATION: PROJECT ELF REQUIRED TWO TRANSMITTER LOCATIONS: ONE IN CLAM LAKE, WISCONSIN, AND THE OTHER IN REPUBLIC, MICHIGAN. THIS CASE FILE FOCUSES ON THE CLAM LAKE FACILITY.

DESCRIPTION: THE USE OF EXTREMELY LOW FREQUENCY WAVES (ALSO KNOWN AS ELF WAVES) HAS BEEN OF INTEREST TO THE UNITED STATES MILITARY FOR OVER HALF A CENTURY. THE PRIMARY OBJECTIVE OF PROJECT ELF WAS TO CREATE A ONE-WAY COMMUNICATION SYSTEM TO RELAY MESSAGES TO AMERICA'S NUCLEAR SUBMARINES. SOME SPECU-LATE THAT ELF WAVES HAVE THE POTENTIAL TO MODIFY THE WEATHER.

WITNESS TESTIMONY: "SOME PEOPLE SEE ELF AS A SIGNIFICANT DETERRENT TO THE TWO WORLD STRUGGLE, A LAST-DITCH MESSEN-GER CENTER FOR SUBMARINES CARRYING NUCLEAR WARHEADS IN CASE AN ATTACK SOMEHOW RENDERED ALL OTHER U.S. DETERRENT FORCES 'INOPERATIVE.' STILL OTHER PEOPLE SEE ELF AS A FIRST STRIKE WEAPON, A SYSTEM DESIGNED TO GIVE THE ORDER FOR U.S. SUBMARINES TO LAUNCH THEIR MISSILES IN AN ALL-OUT SURPRISE OFFENSIVE." LEO HERTZEL, 1981

CONCLUSION: PROJECT ELF WAS OFFICIALLY DISCONTINUED IN 2004. SPECULATION CONTINUES RELATED TO THE FULL EXTENT OF PROJECT ELF'S MILITARY APPLICATIONS.

Fig. 13. Pro–Project ELF activist Jerry Holter (left in vest) poses alongside Captain Charles Beale (far right), John A. Levine (in bowtie), and unidentified men outside the Project ELF facility in Clam Lake, Wisconsin, 1981. Courtesy of the Wisconsin Historical Society—WHi-83127.

Sometimes we only think the sky is falling, but other times it actually is. The latter of which proved true on the afternoon of July 4, 1977, when a severe thunderstorm ensured that fireworks were only the second most likely reason to peer up at the Wisconsin skies. The thunderstorm and accompanying winds cut a 17-mile-wide swath of damage nearly 170 miles in length, wiping out portions of Sawyer, Price, and Oneida counties. Dozens of homes were lost, and hundreds of thousands of acres of forestland were damaged. "The winds reached 100 mph at the Rhinelander airport at about 3:30 p.m.," the National Weather Service reported, "before the instruments blew away."

Such a destructive downburst was rare for the region, and in its aftermath, people became curious as to its cause.

Was it simply a naturally occurring weather phenomenon?

Or was it possible we'd created it ourselves?

By 1977, the notion of weaponizing the weather was hardly a new concept. Since the 1940s the U.S. government and private industries had overseen various experiments related to weather modification. As our capabilities grew, so too did the military's interest. While weather modifications can be used for innocuous purposes—from storm prevention to increasing precipitation in drought-stricken areas—it can also be adapted for the battlefield.

And from 1967 to 1972, it was.

Operation Popeye, as it was known, became the U.S. military's top secret ally in the sky. Not a bombing campaign, but the 54th Weather Reconnaissance Squadron's highly classified mission to ionize clouds over Vietnam through a process called "cloud seeding." By seeding clouds with silver iodide, the military found it could create rainfall with 82 percent accuracy, dramatically disrupting America's adversaries' ground transport capabilities in the process.

Fearing a potential escalation of weather-related warfare, in May of 1977—just two months prior to Wisconsin's severe thunderstorm—the United Nations took the proactive step of signing a treaty banning environmental modification techniques, including weather modification, noting that such manipulation "could have effects extremely harmful to human welfare."

They were right. And that was the end of it.

Maybe.

*

In the summer of 1969—while Operation Popeye was carried out high above the skies of Vietnam—half the world away in Park Falls, Wisconsin, people begin noticing unexplainable disturbances in their telephones lines: hums, buzzes, and the occasional phone ringing of its own volition. Television sets, meanwhile, had developed their own problem: reception regularly lost to static. Under normal circumstances, such minor inconveniences might have been easily resolved with a call to the telephone company or an adjustment to the bunny ears. But since the previous year, the citizens of northern Wisconsin had begun to learn just how abnormal their circumstances really were. Suddenly the North Woods were more than a mecca for outdoor enthusiasts. To everyone's surprise, as a result of a top secret military project called Project Sanguine, the North Woods had become, as its critics put it, "the trigger-finger for World War III."

What exactly was Project Sanguine?

To the antiwar, antinuclear establishment, it was an example of military overreach the likes of which the country had rarely seen. Even by today's standards, the plan seemed wildly ambitious, originally calling for the utilization of somewhere between a third to a half of Wisconsin's lands to create a baseline system of underground cables. In addition, the plan also involved the construction of a series of transmitters, antennas, auxiliary power units, as well as the military facility itself.

And for what purpose?

To create a one-way communication system to relay messages to America's nuclear submarines by way of extremely low frequency waves—better known as ELF waves.

For many, the plan seemed ludicrous. Not only due to its obscene price tag (between 1968 and 1980, Congress appropriated over $146 million to various ELF projects), but also due to the feasibility of its implementation (could we really lay that much line?), as well as larger questions pertaining to the country's need for it.

The use of ELF waves was unique in that they relied upon frequencies that other waves couldn't, thereby allowing them to penetrate rock and earth and the ocean's surface with relative ease and secrecy. Northern Wisconsin had been selected for the project due to its unique geological make up: miles upon miles of low-conductivity rock known as the Laurentian Shield. As a navy spokesman put it in 1969, "To achieve our objective, building a single transmitter complex within the United States that will provide worldwide communications coverage, there is no equally suitable site."

Despite these ideal geological conditions, as well as its vast associated infrastructure, Project Sanguine was never intended to send specific directives to the fleet. Rather, it was meant merely to serve as a "bell-ringer signal" to notify submarines that further communication was required. That's right: all of this to convey the message that further messages needed to be shared. Think of it a beeper on the belt loop of America's submarine fleet: when it buzzed, you knew to make a call.

If your head's spinning, you're not alone. Admittedly, it's a lot to take in. Adding to the complexity was the fact that from 1968 to 1978, the plan changed regularly. Beginning with Project Sanguine (a "survivable and redundant network of antenna grids with approximately 100 transmitters" write Drs. Lowell Klessig and Victor Stite in *The ELF Odyssey*), to the more simplified Project Seafarer ("the non-survivable and much less redundant network of antenna grids with only five transmitters"). In 1973 the project evolved once more to become Project ELF—a proposed communication system that relied on two facilities (one in Clam Lake, Wisconsin, the other in Republic, Michigan), three transmitters, and 160 miles of antenna.

Though this scaled-back version was but a shadow of the navy's originally proposed project, the project's critics remained strenuously opposed, most notably environmentalists and antinuclear activists. But the opposition soon grew to include others as well, including representatives from the North Woods' resort industry, many of whom expressed concerns related to the negative impact the navy's proposed project might have on the region's tourism industry. Native Americans, too, showed some resistance, and were particularly perturbed when Clam Lake resident and pro-ELF advocate Jerry Holter put his woodcarving skills to use by carving a statue of a native figure he named "Chief Sanguine" who, at a push of a button, regaled visitors with the chief's so-called pro-ELF views.

By comparison, the pro-ELF supporters are easier to categorize, their motives most often linked to the project's potential for job creation, as well as their sense of patriotic duty. For many Clam Lake residents, these appeals were enough for them to offer their unequivocal support.

There were jobs to be had and a country in peril.

What more did North Woods citizens need to know?

*

Upon driving into Clam Lake, I spot something entirely unexpected: flashing signs warning me that I've entered an "Elk Crossing Area." Elk are rare in Wisconsin, though not so in Clam Lake. In 1995 the Wisconsin Department of Natural Resources, in partnership with the Rocky Mountain Elk Foundation, relocated 25 elk to the million plus acres of the Chequamegon-Nicolet National Forest. Today, Clam Lake boasts a herd 165 strong, a 4:1 elk to human ratio.

These numbers are impressive, though it's the linguistic coincidence that I can't overlook: how the two features that Clam Lake is known for— ELF and elk—are separated by a single letter. Even more interesting is how one made way for the other. The Clam Lake region was selected for the elk's relocation, in part, due to the cutaways where the twenty-eight-mile-long Project ELF antennas once stood. According to the Forest Service, these open areas were expected to serve as important corridors for the newly introduced elk population, a hypothesis that has since proved true.

Yet I've made the two-hour drive from Eau Claire to Clam Lake not for its elk, but for its ELF. Entering Deb's Y-Go-By Bar & Bait—one of the handful of local businesses on Clam Lake's main drag—I immediately spot sixty-two-year-old Clam Lake historian Lynne Rice perched on a stool at the front of the bar. A lifelong resident, Lynne understands the town and its people better than most. Over the years, she's had a front row seat to Projects Sanguine, Seafarer, and ELF, though I'm most excited to hear her personal story: what it's like being the daughter of Jerry Holter, Clam Lake's pro-ELF spokesperson. Though Jerry passed in 2007, his memory remains strong inside Deb's Y-Go-By Bar & Bait—a property that once served as his general store and gas station.

"See that trim?" Lynne says, pointing me to the thin strip just above the jukebox. "Dad did that."

Lynne and I relocate to the back of the bar, where we're soon joined by two others who knew Jerry well—eighty-one-year-old Pat Reinders, a long-time Clam Lake resident herself, and sixty-four-year-old Tom Biasi, who worked for Project ELF from 1993 to 2005, when the project closed.

"Jerry was a great PR guy," Tom says. "He just had that gift."

It was a gift that came with practice. After a quarter century selling cars in Chippewa Falls, Wisconsin, in 1969 Jerry and his family uprooted to Clam Lake, where his salesmanship skills soon translated to selling fellow citizens on the importance of Projects Sanguine, Seafarer, and eventually, ELF. Moreover, as the proprietor of Clam Lake's gas station and general store—a social gathering place for residents—Jerry regularly positioned himself on the front lines of any and all conversations pertaining to the navy's projects. On occasion, navy representatives dropped by the general store themselves, wowing local residents with their stories. Though just fifteen years old in 1969, Lynne vividly recalls long afternoons spent making malts and sundaes for store patrons, hardly aware of the highly secretive project taking place just a few miles from her family's store.

"I was just a kid, I wasn't thinking about ELF," Lynne laughs. "I was just thinking about boys."

From 1969 to 2005, the navy's presence—as well as the anti-ELF protestors that accompanied it—became part of the normal routine for Clam Lake residents. Yet Jerry, who never missed an opportunity to spin a story, often took it upon himself to give protestors an experience that was anything but normal. When protestors stopped into the store to ask for directions to the Project ELF facility, Jerry put his storytelling skills to use, concocting wild tales involving the last batch of unwanted protestors who'd dared protest the facility. More often than not—according to Jerry, that is—those poor protestors were chased by hungry bears.

Pat and Tom laugh as Lynne concludes her father's story.

"That's Jerry, all right," Pat confirms. "There was never a dull moment with him."

*

At the height of the controversies surrounding Project ELF, dull moments were indeed in short supply. On October 1, 1989, after over twenty years of studies and tests, Clam Lake's Wisconsin Transmitter

Facility, home to Project ELF, officially began sending signals to a second transmitter in Republic, Michigan, who then relayed the signals to U.S. subs.

Mission—at long last—accomplished.

For the pro-ELF contingent, the system seemed entirely reasonable—a safe mechanism to communicate to submarines without foreign interference. Yet ELF opposition—especially those protesting on antiwar and antinuclear grounds—feared not only the communication system but also the types of communications that might be sent.

"Some people see ELF as a significant deterrent to the two world struggle, a last-ditch messenger center for submarines carrying nuclear warheads in case an attack somehow rendered all other U.S. deterrent forces 'inoperative,'" Leo Hertzel wrote in a 1981 article. "Still other people see ELF as a first strike weapon, a system designed to give the order for U.S. submarines to launch their missiles in an all-out surprise offensive."

So which was it? A nuclear deterrent or one giant step toward nuclear annihilation?

Local residents couldn't help but wonder what housing such a facility might mean for them. If Clam Lake served as a relay point for a nuclear strike directive, did that mean Clam Lake opened itself up to a retaliatory strike? Had they placed themselves in the Soviet's crosshairs?

"While there is no way of knowing what priority an aggressor might attach to a potential target," a navy representative informed locals in 1969, "it is unlikely that he would place a high priority on a single communications facility knowing that even if he did destroy it he would not destroy our communications capability. It certainly would not seem to warrant the same priority as other more vital facilities."

Translation: since we could relay the message by other means, obliterating Clam Lake, not to mention a good chunk of the Chequamegon-Nicolet National Forest, probably wasn't worth the trouble.

I wonder if such sentiments eased local residents' concerns; according to Pat, they did.

"If they were going to drop a nuke on anything it would be a big city, not a military facility here in the woods," Pat explains. "You could deal with us in other ways."

Sabotage certainly would have proved more cost-effective, and according to a 1979 report from the General Accounting Office, the facility was, indeed, vulnerable to such an attack. In fact, according to the General Accounting Office, even a less nefarious plot—one involving a tree on an overhead ELF line, for instance—might've been enough to disrupt the entire system. Such infiltration possibilities were surely an embarrassment for the navy, who'd invested tens of millions of dollars in the technology itself. Despite all the extensive scientific testing, there was simply no quick fix for the threat of a forest's worth of trees. U.S. intelligence agencies could guard against the threat of Soviet saboteurs, but who could protect Project ELF from a jack pine in a windstorm?

Despite these setbacks, most Clam Lake residents remained committed to the cause.

Including Pat Reinders, who—while seated around the table at Deb's Y-Go-By—informs me that in the early 1970s, she and Lynne's mother, Tish Holter, were dispatched to various naval bases (three times to Naval Station Great Lakes in Chicago, Illinois; twice to the Naval Air Station in Pensacola) for three days of rigorous medical testing. Anti-ELF protestors had long claimed that ELF waves had the potential to pose health risks to humans, and the navy hoped to dispel such myths. And who better to test than local residents who lived and worked in close proximity?

"What were those tests like?" I ask Pat.

"It was like having the best physical exam ever," she says.

"What were they looking for?"

"Anomalies," Pat shrugs.

"Did they find any?"

"Not to my knowledge."

Pat describes the tests as "quite extensive," recalling one that sent a light shock rippling through her leg to test her reflexes. "I felt like a frog," she laughs, "but it was nothing we couldn't handle."

Lynne opens a binder to reveal a photograph of her mother and Pat frolicking in Pensacola Bay in the midst of one of their testing trips.

"How old are you there?" I ask Pat.

"Oh, I guess we were in our thirties."

An age when the ability to jet set from Clam Lake to Florida had proved quite alluring for the young women. Not only could they spend half a week trading the Wisconsin winter for the Sunshine State, but they could also fulfill what, for them, felt like their patriotic duty.

Having grown up in a navy family, Pat felt a deep sense of duty toward her country, and when called upon to endure five years of testing, she readily agreed. Making herself the navy's guinea pig was the best way she knew to silence the squawking from anti-ELF protestors. If the tests revealed that she was, in fact, a healthy, cancer-free, non-glow-in-the-dark human, then the protestors "human health concerns" argument would be dramatically undercut.

"I felt [the protestors] had a perfect right to have their say," Pat tells me, weighing her words carefully, "but they didn't have a perfect right to make up facts." According to Pat, playing fast and loose with the facts served as a central component of the anti-ELF strategy.

"Sling it against the wall and see what sticks," she says. "And that's what a lot of it was. 'You're going to be sterile, the trout are gone.' Without the facts to prove it, they could just toss anything against the wall. That's the only thing I objected to. Protest, protest peaceful," she agrees, "but know your facts. And don't swallow everything that someone says without checking up."

In part, that's why Pat had agreed to the tests in the first place.

"I wanted to know the facts," Pat says, "and I figured if I was part of the tests, I'd know them."

Early in their public relations campaign, the navy had issued a similar warning, urging local residents to take the time to understand the many nuances of the project rather than rush to judgment.

"Our interest is in assuring that [Project Sanguine] is as well understood as possible," a navy representative assured residents at a public meeting in 1969, "primarily because those people who understand it best are least concerned."

It was a statement several scientists took issue with, many of whom claimed that it was difficult to understand the proposed project whatsoever given the many unknowns surrounding the long-term effects of ELF waves. One of its main critics was Ashland College's Dr. Lowell Klessig, who, after dedicating years of study to the proposed projects—and even cowriting a book on the subject—remained leerier than ever of the navy's plans.

On March 12, 1974, the twenty-nine-year-old professor expressed his concerns at a public meeting in Michigan. "One of the big problems I've found in the five years I've been working on Sanguine is that there are not a lot of answers," he explained to the crowd. "And so any time you go to speak on a topic where you don't know all the answers and someone else says they know the answers or at least they may know the answers but they're hiding them behind a stamp marked 'Classified'—well, it's very difficult. It's almost like fighting with a ghost behind a partially transparent net."

The "they" was a direct shot at navy representatives, who despite offering lip service related to transparency, had, in the opinions of many, failed to achieve that aim. The navy's secrecy was indisputable. In fact, it's hard to know if and when they might have disclosed Project Sanguine were it not for a Wisconsin congressman named Alvin O'Konski who, much to the navy's frustration, declassified the project during a reelection campaign. Equally damning, at least to Klessig, was the navy's attempt to classify any and all newspaper reports (hence, the "behind a stamp marked 'Classified'" jab) that made mention of the project.

Neither of these actions reaffirmed the navy's stated promise of transparency.

"Ask yourself," Klessig said to the crowd, "how much [does the navy] care about an ordinary citizen from Wisconsin or Texas or Michigan? How much do they care about informing that person what they plan to do? In my opinion, they care zero."

Under pressure from Wisconsin Senator Gaylord Nelson (who himself had not been briefed on the project, even during his time as the state's governor), the navy attempted to deal with their mounting transparency problems by contracting Hazleton Laboratories to run an environmental impact study on the proposed Project Sanguine. It was their hope that Hazleton's findings might lay to rest at least some of the many environmental questions and rumors propagated by ELF's opponents.

Though the Hazleton study didn't reveal any smoking guns, it did acknowledge that the enormous antenna would certainly impact humans, animals, and plant life, all of which would be "exposed to its fields for very long periods of time unless they are killed by it, are removed, or, in the case of the free-ranging animals, are driven out by noxious effects."

Hardly a ringing endorsement.

Yet of most interest to Klessig was a paragraph tucked deep within the navy's contract with Hazleton, one noting that "evidence should be given that individuals assigned will subordinate their own interest and will take directions from Navy project managers who may have little knowledge of biological science."

For ELF opponents, the statement reeked of a tail-wagging-the-dog situation, immediately calling into question the validity and independence of the results. Dr. Klessig also disputed Hazleton's findings on what he perceived as shoddy science. "If I had a graduate student who turned in that kind of work to me as a class project," he remarked, "the student couldn't get a passing grade."

Facts had been called for and facts had been tendered, but the two sides were no closer to consensus. So much remained unknown.

And when the downburst storm struck on July 4, 1977, the plot only thickened further.

*

In February of 1981, John Stauber and Craig Kronstedt of STOP Project ELF—an organization whose mission it was, you guessed it, to halt the ELF project—held a press conference in the Wisconsin state capitol.

As the reporters reached for their notepads, Stauber and Kronstedt offered what for many seemed an impossible claim: that ELF waves emanating from the Clam Lake facility may have had spurred the July 4, 1977, thunderstorm. "The Navy's ELF system may have inadvertently triggered a weather bomb," Stauber stated. "An inspection of the facility's operating logs shows a direct correlation between the time the transmission went on at full power and the intensity of the storm."

Based on research from the University of Chicago, STOP Project ELF representatives posited that it was possible that, as they put it, the "pulsating field of the ELF antenna signal could create and modulate the ions in a cloud alternately attracting and repelling them. If enough ionization occurred an avalanche of ions could trigger a downburst."

It made for an interesting theory, one that blamed ELF waves for the kind of cloud seeding that had typically been done by aircraft. An issue of the Madison-based *ECO Bulletin* noted, too, that the July 4 downburst had displayed "several unusual characteristics."

"It was not steady but rather pulsated as it moved along its 166 mile swath, hitting and then releasing, hitting and releasing as many as 25 times. Even more unusual," the article continued, "is that the storm swung in an almost semi-circular path around the Navy's ELF antenna."

Such claims only raised further questions pertaining to causation and correlation. Was the downburst *caused* by the ELF waves, or were the two events correlative in nature?

The *ECO Bulletin* was quick to note that though the circumstantial evidence "does not prove that ELF causes storms . . . it does suggest that ELF may have the capacity to attract and intensify already present storm systems."

Was it true?

Had the ELF facility in Clam Lake, Wisconsin, weaponized the weather?

For four weeks in 1981, STOP Project ELF representatives John Stauber and Jenny Speicher attempted to find out. Following a successful request for documents under the Freedom of Information Act, the pair hunkered down in navy offices in Washington DC, combing through what Stauber later estimated to be "hundreds of thousands of pages of materials." They piled what they hoped to have copied, but according to Stauber, a portion of their selected documents never made it back into their hands. "There were fascinating records that were relative to problems they were having with the operation of the [Wisconsin] Test Facility in the weeks before and after the downburst storm," Stauber claimed. "They were having all sorts of bizarre problems trying to get their system up and operating. We were never able to get those documents out of there."

With no documentation to support their claim, Stauber feared that STOP Project ELF would never find the necessary traction to propel a wider investigation into their weather modification theory. Decades later, he admitted regretting having broached the subject at all. Though he believed STOP Project ELF representatives were asking legitimate questions, the questions were, as Stauber put it, "simply impossible to answer." With little science to support it—and even fewer internal documents to confirm it—he knew it appeared as if they were grasping at straws.

"It was something that really won us a lot of ridicule," he said.

As noted previously, STOP Project ELF had based its theory on ELF-induced weather modifications as a result of having read the facility's logbooks. But Stanley Kasieta, the director of the Clam Lake facility at the time, strongly disputed the claim.

"It's a lot of baloney," he said in a 1981 interview. "[STOP Project ELF representatives] didn't even read the log right when they looked at it. They didn't even understand that the log is in Zulu time, Greenwich time, and they thought it was in local time so their times are all wrong."

Both sides further entrenched themselves, making any attempt at agreement seem all the more out of reach. While STOP Project ELF newsletters listed an array of harmful biological effects as a result of ELF waves (everything from bone tumors, to weight gain, to sterility), the pro-ELF contingent accused their opposition of purposefully misleading the public for their own ends.

"These people are anti-everything," Stanley Kasieta remarked. "They're anti-military, anti-nuclear power, they're for unilateral disarmament. Yes, I suppose they're environmentalists too but that's not so important. Right now, they just want print. That's why they thought up that story about the storm."

What once might have been described as an honest disagreement among concerned citizens had grown to become much more. The debate had turned fiercely personal. How you felt was who you were.

The more I learn about Projects Sanguine, Seafarer, and ELF, the more I wonder if these military projects were a proxy war for the era's larger issues pertaining to civil unrest. Specifically, if the declassification of Project Sanguine in 1968 added fuel to an already burning fire. Ostensibly, Project Sanguine's antiwar and antinuclear protestors appeared to be debating the use of extremely low frequency waves for military purposes. But beneath that particular debate loomed a larger one, one that challenged the zeitgeist of the time.

What, after all, did it mean to be an American in the late 1960s? Who were we? What did we stand for? And what did we stand against?

*

Perhaps it all comes down to facts. Or rather, the facts one chooses to believe.

As you've surely gleaned, nothing about the navy's ELF projects is easy to understand. The shroud of secrecy has since dissipated, though there's still plenty that remains unknown. Dr. Klessig's 1974 statement about fighting a "ghost behind a partially transparent net" seems as true as ever. Even with more information now available, unless one's earned the proper degrees, that information isn't terribly helpful. While those for and against the use of ELF waves have long accused one another of spreading misinformation, the public's struggle to grasp the topic is likely linked to the technical nature of the information itself. After all, ELF waves are beyond our perception. We can't see them, we can't hear them, and according to most, we can't even feel their presence. But that doesn't mean they're not there.

In a 1994 interview Jerry Holter confirmed that the majority of people—even regionally—had little understanding of Project ELF. "They don't really know. They haven't taken it upon themselves to make a study of it. Which is only normal for the American people, they could care less, they've got their things to do. Why worry about a little ELF Project out here in Clam Lake, Wisconsin?"

As people began coming down one way or the other on the use of ELF waves, the facts, complex as they were, were often dwarfed by self-interest: what individuals felt they had to lose or gain. And most of the folks in Clam Lake believed there was plenty to gain, Jerry estimating that 99 percent of locals were in favor of the Clam Lake facility. A job was a job, after all, and for a region that rarely courted new industries, the navy's projects seemed too enticing to pass up. For many, the prospect of improving one's financial situation seemed worth the risk of the many unsubstantiated fears.

"Everyone worked there," Lynne Rice says from our place around the table at Deb's Y-Go-By.

"Best paying job around," Pat agrees.

Tom, who worked at the facility for over a decade, confirms that the job was hard to beat: year-round and with benefits.

But despite these firsthand accounts, as well as Jerry's 99 percent estimate, a 1981 referendum painted a different picture. The question—"Do you favor having Project ELF in Ashland County: Yes or No?"—resulted in 50.7 percent of Ashland County voters voting yes, with 49.3 percent voting no.

I ask Lynne, Pat, and Tom about this disconnect: How could 99 percent of Clam Lake locals be in favor of Project ELF as Jerry had estimated, when a countywide referendum revealed such vastly different numbers?

None of them know for sure, though they do note that despite Clam Lake's small population, the land is divided into several counties, with Ashland County being the most progressive.

I hear where they're coming from, though it's a difficult claim to accept. How could the perspectives from the people in Clam Lake be so sharply at odds with the perspectives of those in the wider region?

"It's hard for me to know what to think about all this," I admit to

Lynne, Pat, and Tom. "For the most part, it seems that there were at least some facts both sides agreed on, and yet how those facts were interpreted . . . what people chose to believe . . . it led to very different conclusions. I guess I don't understand how."

"Well, isn't that how it's always been?" Pat asks. "Religion, politics, you name it. I think it's the nature of the beast."

Perhaps she's right. After all, our desire to cherry-pick the facts is hardly a new idea. Perhaps, too, our willingness to put our feelings *before* the facts further contributes to the creation of this beast—one that thrives on confirming our beliefs rather than asking us to think critically about them. In an attempt to placate the beast, we feed it only what it wants. And once it's got a taste for what it likes, why bother with anything else?

*

Project ELF officially operated in Clam Lake, Wisconsin, for fifteen years before shuttering its doors in 2004. Having spent but a few hours in Clam Lake myself, it's hard for me to gauge any long-term effects on its people or habitat. Did the trout streams dry up? Was the flora and fauna affected? Certainly, there are more elk than there were before, and for some locals, that's proof enough of Project ELF's positive impact on the region. Today, Clam Lake residents are proud to be known as the "Elk Capital of Wisconsin," a claim to fame far less controversial than the one bestowed upon them by STOP Project ELF: "the trigger finger for World War III."

As we stand to say our goodbyes, Lynne turns to me and says, "You know, Dad's probably jumping for joy over at the cemetery. He'd love to know Project ELF is getting a little more press."

I smile—happy to shed a little light on a subject that for so long has been shrouded in shadows.

"While I'm here," I say, "I think I'll drive out to the old facility. See what's left of the place."

"Well there's not much," Lynne says as we head toward our vehicles. "But good luck out there." She smiles. "And watch out for any lingering rays!"

*

Following a 1970s-era navy map courtesy of Lynne, I eventually find my way down the unmarked road that leads me to the remains of the facility. After a ten-minute drive past several "Pavement Ends" signs, I eventually crunch my tires to a halt before a locked wooden gate at the edge of the road. It's peculiar—a gate that appears to protect nothing but the overgrowth stretched before me. Back at Deb's Y-Go-By, Lynne had shared with me a recent aerial photo of the property, which showed the land wiped clean of the main building. From my place at the edge of the gate, all I can make out are the trees, the flowers, and the wild reclaiming the land. Standing there, I try to imagine the protestors. And I try, too, to imagine the employees who passed the guard house every day on the way to work inside the facility. I think back to the storm of 1977 and wonder: *Did that originate here, too? Did someone crank the dials a little too high? Employ* ELF *waves to create a downburst by mistake?*

Likely not. At least given the evidence I've seen.

But even more difficult to imagine is the confirmable fact: how once, many years back, this humble landscape might've relayed the message for nuclear war, the signal traveling from Clam Lake, Wisconsin, to Republic, Michigan, then on to the submarines.

I think: *This is where the end of the world might've begun.*

It's a truth too hard to fathom, and one I'm unwilling to face. Though we lived to see that future, we mightn't have had the wrong message passed through the cables.

Shuddering, I walk back to my vehicle, start the engine, then return to the world that remains.

The Kensington Runestone

1362(?)–Present

NAME: THE KENSINGTON RUNESTONE

SCIENTIFIC NAME: N/A

LOCATION: KENSINGTON, MINNESOTA

DESCRIPTION: IN 1898 A FARMER UNEARTHED A SLAB OF GRAYWACKE STONE UPON WHICH WAS INSCRIBED AN ANCIENT RUNIC MESSAGE DATED 1362. IF AUTHENTIC, THIS STONE MIGHT FOREVER ALTER OUR UNDERSTANDING OF NORTH AMERICA'S DISCOVERY. IF A HOAX, THEN WHO PERPETRATED IT?

WITNESS TESTIMONY: "FEW QUESTIONS IN AMERICAN HISTORY HAVE STIRRED SO MUCH CURIOSITY OR PROVOKED SUCH EXTENDED DISCUS- SIONS AS THAT OF THE AUTHENTICITY OF THE RUNIC INSCRIPTION ON A STONE FOUND NEAR KENSINGTON, MINNESOTA, IN 1898." THEODORE BLEGEN, 1968

CONCLUSION: THIS CONTROVERSY CONTINUES.

In 1898 forty-four-year-old Swedish immigrant Olof Ohman was clear- ing land on his farm near Kensington, Minnesota, when he came upon a tree that refused to budge. After much effort he worked it free with a winch, felling the aspen and finding the source of the trouble beneath: a large slab of graywacke stone gripped between its roots.

Weighing in at 202 pounds, and with dimensions of thirty inches tall, sixteen inches wide, and six inches thick, the stone was a rare find. But Ohman, who had much work to do, paid little attention to the discovery.

Fig. 14. The Kensington Runestone. Courtesy of the Runestone Museum.

It wasn't until his ten-year-old son Edward bent down for a closer look that the stone's secrets began to reveal themselves. Brushing away the dirt, Edward noticed strange markings carved into the stone's outer layer.

Edward hollered to his father, who upon inspecting the markings himself, became equally baffled.

What could the markings possibly mean? And who had made them?

As word of the discovery spread throughout the village of Kensington (population two hundred or so), the Ohmans soon became begrudging hosts to several shovel-wielding treasure hunters—none of whom found anything of note. Perhaps because the greatest treasure had already been unearthed: an alleged fourteenth-century runestone that, if authentic, would forever alter our understanding of North America's discovery.

Today, there's no question about the Norse colonization of North America in the late tenth century. This became particularly clear following the discovery of a pair of Viking settlements in eastern Canada: Vinland and L'Anse aux Meadows. However, the question that remains is: Just how deep into America's mainland did Norse explorers go? Following their settlements in eastern Canada, did the explorers simply continue heading west? Is it possible they sailed through the Hudson Bay and down the Red River into, dare I say it, west central Minnesota?

It all depends on if you believe the authenticity of the runestone inscription, which reads as follows:

Eight Goths and 22 Norsemen on (an) exploration-journey from Vinland through the western regions. We had camp by 2 skerries one day's journey north from this stone. We were (out) and fished one day. When we came home (we) found ten men, red with blood and dead. Ave Maria! Save (us) from evil. (We) have ten of our party by the sea to look after (or for) our vessels 14 day journey from this island. Year 1362.

Translation: the explorers came, they saw, and they did not conquer. In fact, according to some interpretations, it appears Native Americans likely conquered them, or at least drove them from the obviously hostile territory. However, others claim the bubonic plague was to blame for the ten men "red with blood and dead."

The cause of the men's deaths is but one of the stone's many mysteries, and perhaps irrelevant if the broader tale fails to be true.

In one sense, the stone's story seems ludicrous: bearded, muscle-bound, axe-wielding explorers wandering the wilds of the Gopher State. Yet in another sense, it seems perfectly logical, too. After all, what was stopping the most capable sailors in the world from traveling a bit further west than we initially thought?

Despite advancements in a range of fields (archeology, linguistics, runic studies, among others), scholars remain split on the stone's authenticity. Even enlisting the support of new technologies—including a 3-D digital microscope—failed to persuade the skeptics. As the past century has proven, there's always some new angle to consider, some new tidbit of information that's been previously overlooked. How old was the tree from which the stone was pulled? Is the stone's weather-ing consistent with the timeline? The questions are endless, leading twentieth-century historian and Kensington Runestone scholar The-odore Blegen to remark that "few questions in American history have stirred so much curiosity or provoked such extended discussions as that of the authenticity of the runic inscription on a stone found near Kensington, Minnesota, in 1898."

Half a century later, Blegen's words remain as true as ever.

To delve deep into the mysteries surrounding the Kensington Rune-stone is to lose oneself in a swirl of runic symbols, cryptograms, Vikings, monks, the Knights of Templar, amid a host of other complicating factors that have fascinated and frustrated scholars for well over a hundred years.

Most frustrating, however, is that on the surface, this seems a simple story: once upon a time a farmer found a stone in his field. Yet following this singular agreed-upon fact, scholars' viewpoints begin to dramat-ically diverge. To this day, we can't even say for certain which month Ohman discovered the stone, let alone come to consensus on the more complicated questions: Who carved it, why did they carve it, and when?

Attempts to answer these questions began in January of 1899, when a Kensington banker sent a copy of the inscription to a Scandinavian linguist from the University of Minnesota. After careful study, the linguist concluded that the runestone was inauthentic. The language employed did not appear to be Old Norse, thereby invalidating any claim of authenticity. Scholars on both sides of the ocean soon verified this initial conclusion.

One mystery was solved—or so it seemed—but another remained: If it was a hoax, then who had done the hoaxing? Much of the suspicion fell to Olof Ohman, who by unearthing the stone had caused far more hubbub than he intended, including implicating himself as the hoaxer. In an attempt to wipe his hands clean of the flap, Ohman placed the stone facedown outside his granary, hopeful it might fade into obscurity and put an end to the trouble once and for all.

It might have, were it not for a thirty-four-year-old Norwegian American historian named Hjalmar Holand, who knocked on the Ohmans' farmhouse door in the summer of 1907.

Hello there, he said, *I've come to see the stone.*

For the rest of his life, it would hang from Holand's neck like an albatross.

*

In a book overflowing with monsters and Martians, it's only logical to ask: So where do we put the stone? We stick it at the end, of course, because a stone isn't nearly as sexy as a werewolf. Yet in terms of strangeness, the stone holds its own: not in an "otherworldly" sense, but in the sense that it requires us to reconsider the world as we know it. What if rugged Norse sailors were the original Lewis and Clark? And what if America's ties to Scandinavia go deeper than we think?

Yet strange, too, is the allure of this particular mystery, which has become for scholars what Charybdis was for sailors—an all-consuming whirlpool that, once it gets you, never lets you go.

As it was for Hjalmar Holand.

After being sucked into the runestone saga in 1907, a stubborn Holand remained transfixed on the mystery until his death in 1963. Of course, one man's albatross is another man's crusade, and for Holand the runestone was perhaps a bit of both. He nonetheless accepted his charge fully, despite the trouble the stone would cause him. Part showman, part scholar, for decades Holand served as the stone's most outspoken advocate. Not only did he defend its authenticity in a series of books, lectures, and tours, but he repopularized the runestone when it seemed all but forgotten.

Holand believed so deeply in the stone's authenticity that he displayed it around the world. For some it was little more than a curiosity, though for others it literally served as nothing short of rock-solid, tangible proof of the pre-Columbian discovery of North America.

In 1948 the stone received the ultimate validation by being displayed at the Smithsonian Institution in Washington DC, allowing onlookers to come to their own conclusions. Adding further credence to the authenticity claim was the assessment offered by Dr. M. W. Stirling, the Smithsonian's director of the Bureau of American Ethnology, who called the runestone "probably the most important archeological object yet found in North America." Stirling wasn't alone. In a private letter to Holand, T. S. Stewart, the Smithsonian's acting head curator in the Department of Anthropology noted that he was "loath to think of the Kensington Stone leaving the halls of the United States National Museum" following the conclusion of the exhibition in 1949.

Personal endorsements by high-profile experts confirmed that opinions on the stone had begun to change. Holand's advocacy played no small part in the matter. Enduring scholars' slings and arrows for much of his lifetime, Holand nevertheless remained firmly committed to the stone's authenticity. He built his case around linguistic, archeological, and historical findings, all of which, for him, confirmed the stone's validity. To Holand, it all made perfect sense: not only did the stone demonstrate the proper usage of ancient runes, but it also told a story that fit neatly within the timeline of Norway and Sweden's King Magnus Eriksson's proposed 1355 expedition to the West. Had the expedition actually been undertaken? And if so, had the Norse sailors ended up in present-day Kensington? Holand believed they had.

In an attempt to buoy his case, Holand pointed critics to additional era-specific artifacts that had been unearthed in and around the site of the stone's discovery, including axes and fire steels. Even more interesting to Holand, however, was the discovery of what he believed to be mooring holes chiseled into nearby rocks. If authentic, the holes would further confirm that boats had been moored to that land centuries before.

Of course, these discoveries came with their controversies. What if the axes and fire steels were simply brought over by later immigrants? And what if the mooring holes were simply drilled by farmers in an attempt to break the stones by way of dynamite sticks?

Critics were quick to dismiss Holand's theories, though few seemed willing to point an unequivocal finger at the stone's alleged forger. Yet when they did, Holand was only too happy to reciprocate such dismissiveness.

"Sooner or later all opponents get around to accusing Ohman," Holand noted in an undated essay. "This has become a necessity with them because the theory of a forgery without a forger is not convincing. It is like an accusation of murder without the victim—the *corpus delecti* must be found."

For decades, people questioned Ohman's motives, morals, and intellect—a continual public probing that took a dramatic toll on the family's well-being. While Kensington residents were quick to defend Ohman, it was never enough to satisfy the naysayers, who believed the most logical answer to "Who's the hoaxer?" was the man who'd found the stone.

In serving as the stone's defender, Holand became Ohman's defender, too. He understood that if Ohman was found guilty—even if only in the court of public opinion—then the authenticity question would become moot. And so, Holand waged a public relations campaign on Ohman's behalf, claiming the Kensington farmer to be a man of "fine, frank dignity" and "the product of clean conscience and a conduct of life that developed true self-respect."

Aside from the flattery, Holand also attempted an entirely different tack: characterizing Ohman as a man lacking the intelligence to pull off such a hoax. "It seems most absurd to assume that Olof Ohman with a scholastic education inferior to that of a fourth grader at present should be able to write a lengthy inscription of more than 200 characters," Holand argued. "Even now, with all our colleagues and learned books there are probably not more than a hundred men in this country who could write their own names in runes."

According to Holand, Ohman was simultaneously too ethical and too inept to manage such a feat.

Raising the question: Who was smart enough—and duplicitous enough—to pull off such a stunt?

*

Rune scholar that I'm not, I'm hardly in a position to come to any definitive answers. Frankly, the deeper I delved into the Kensington Runestone mystery, the more convoluted it became. As scholars have proven for over a century, even when one possesses expertise in the field, it's difficult to reach a conclusion. For a guy like me, whose knowledge of Old Norse is sorely lacking, any chance of a break in the case seemed unlikely.

One day, after a bleary-eyed marathon session working through the Hjalmar and Harold Holand Papers at the archive, I pushed the piles of paper aside and began plotting my 450-mile roundtrip journey to Kensington, Minnesota. If I wanted answers, I needed to look beyond the papers and the books and go to the land itself. The land where once, Norse explorers carved (or did not carve) their story into stone.

I filled up my gas tank, buckled my belt, then set my coordinates for the runestone.

*

Throughout the early twentieth century, as scholars continued to point the finger toward Olof Ohman, Dr. Julius Olson, Scandinavian languages professor at the University of Wisconsin, pointed elsewhere. In a series of letters written to Minnesota Historical Society secretary

Warren Upham in the spring of 1910, Dr. Olson proclaimed that he had a strong suspicion who the guilty man was, and his name wasn't Ohman.

"He has all the qualifications for the perpetuation of a forgery like the Kensington inscription," Dr. Olson wrote to Upham. "I can *prove absolutely* that he has studied a book that treats of runes and *contains the runic numbers.*"

The stone's usage of rare runic numbers was, for many experts, proof of its authenticity. After all, few people in the world possessed such specialized knowledge, let alone someone from the region. But if such a man could be found, Dr. Olson hypothesized, then it was likely he was the forger.

Moreover, according to Dr. Olson, only one book offered the detailed runic numeral information needed to perpetuate the hoax: *Fasti Danici*, a rather obscure 1643 text by Danish physician and antiquarian Ole Worm.

Dr. Olson came across the rare book while browsing the library at the University of Wisconsin, at which point he began to wonder: Who else's fingerprints might be on it?

Limiting the list of suspects further was the fact that the volume was written in Latin, meaning the alleged hoaxer not only needed access to this very book, but also required fluency in the dead language.

Writing to a friend and fellow scholar in May of 1910, Dr. Olson laid out his case.

"Now, while turning over the pages of Fasti Danici I happened to think of a Norwegian student who graduated at the University here in the early '80s," and who had "devoted much time to the study of Scandinavian antiquities."

During his time at the university this student had also taken it upon himself to organize the books in the Scandinavian language department's library, a task that gave him access to *Fasti Danici*. For Dr. Olson, the smoking gun wasn't the mere *possibility* that the student in question had access to the book, but an article in which the student himself confirmed his knowledge of *Fasti Danici*.

That student was Ole E. Hagen.

After emigrating to America in 1869, Hagen studied for two years at Galesville University before enrolling in the University of Wisconsin in 1878. Four years later, he earned a pair of bachelor's degrees (one in arts, the other in literature) before returning to Galesville to teach. By 1884 the University of Wisconsin granted him two additional master's degrees, at which point he took his studies overseas, furthering his expertise in language studies by earning his doctorate at Germany's Leipzig University. Throughout the late 1880s, his scholarship took him to the British Museum, the Louvre, and the Royal Museum in Berlin.

But this is where Hagen's timeline grows murky. We know he returned to America to accept a professorship at the University of South Dakota in 1891, though what's less clear is where he was in the months preceding his appointment.

"Where was he during the year before Sept. 1891?" Dr. Olson asked in a letter to his friend. "That is what I have been trying to find out."

In an effort to do so, Dr. Olson reached out once more to Upham, hopeful that together, they might find a way to ascertain the much-needed information. In a letter dated May 4, 1910, Upham offered to send a "trustworthy reputed land buyer or agent" to "incidentally talk with Prof. Hagen about Minnesota lands, etc., especially in southwestern Douglas County, where Kensington is, to secure thus any possible evidence looking toward his being a forger of this."

Dr. Olson and Upham believed that if they could get Hagen to admit his familiarity with the region in which the stone was discovered, then they'd be one step closer to confirming their suspicions. The plan would have been put into motion were it not for a last minute conflict with the agent in question who, for reasons unknown, was unable to complete his task.

Though Dr. Olson's allegations remained mostly in the confines of private letters, evidence points to such suspicions dogging Hagen for years. Despite possessing one of the most scholarly minds in the region, Hagen's academic career at the University of South Dakota—which lasted from 1891 to 1908, with one year off in between—was plagued with discontentment. Cedric Cummins's early history of the University of South Dakota highlights Hagen's troubles in Vermillion, most of which were spurred by a feud between Hagen and a colleague in the College of

Commerce. Ultimately, the Board of Regents asked both men to resign, putting an abrupt end to Hagen's academic career.

It was under these trying circumstances that Hagen and his family resettled in Rock Falls, Wisconsin. Having spent his formative years there, Hagen knew the area well, and was enticed back due to the close proximity to his mother and brother. The family moved onto a property dubbed Lilac Lane Farm and together looked forward to a life far removed from the quarrels of academia. Or so Hagen hoped.

According to historian Theodore Blegen, Hagen made a smooth transition from scholar to "scholar-farmer," noting that Hagen remained "busy with his pen on his farm" until shortly before his death on January 1, 1927. Scholar-farmer that he was, Rock Falls locals knew Hagen simply as "Prof," a term of endearment that acknowledged his accomplishments.

When he wasn't tending livestock or spending time with his family, Hagen could often be found putting his linguistic knowledge to good use, including a careful study of the Kensington Runestone's inscription—the inscription he himself was accused of having forged. Was his interest in the inscription a means to clear his name? Or, as Dr. Olson may have believed, simply more smoke and mirrors to throw others off his scent?

In 1924, after years of study, Hagen promised to soon make his findings public. Yet in 1926, his home was consumed by fire, burning much of his library—and his life's work—along with it.

Neighbors and friends speculated that the fire broke him, one final blow to add to the list of previous hardships Hagen had endured, including the death of his eight-year-old son, Leif, as well as the untimely end of his college teaching career. He informed his friend, newspaperman Waldemar Ager, that without his papers he could only offer a "categorical statement" pertaining to the Kensington Runestone. His statement: he—much like Hjalmar Holand—could find nothing definitive to prove the stone a hoax.

"I worked over the stone for a whole day under different kinds of light and found the runes on the whole to be what I looked for from that time and the people that are mentioned in the inscription."

Though he declined to take a definitive stance, he leaned toward authenticity.

"My advice is therefore," Hagen concluded, "that the Kensington stone be placed in a safe repository where it can be preserved as an important epigraphic document concerning American History."

Today that "safe repository" is the Runestone Museum in Alexandria, Minnesota, which I visit one warm fall morning. After driving 225 miles, I fork over the eight-dollar admission fee and enter through the museum's closed doors. At last, I am face to face with the final stop on my year of living strangely: a stone whose strangeness exists solely by the story it refuses to tell.

There it is, standing upright behind glass, a single hanging light cast over it.

Sure, it might be North America's greatest archeological find, but it might also be nothing more than the handiwork of a trickster with a chisel.

Staring at the stone, I consider the many hands that have come into contact with it: the original inscriber for starters (whoever he or they were), as well as Olof Ohman who raised it from the ground, Hjalmar Holand who took it on the road, and Ole Hagen who read its runes for clues. They've all played a role in untangling this tale, yet plenty of tangles remain.

I study the stone, observing it from all angles, none of which offer me any new information.

If stones could talk, I think as I press my face to the glass, *what might this one say?*

*

It's a lot, I know, so allow me to offer the short version:

Once upon a time a farmer found a stone in his field, and then, all hell broke loose.

For a century, scholars of all stripes have offered their opinions, none of which have been proven definitively. The archeologists weighed in, as did the linguists, and the geologists, and the mineralogists, and the historians, and the anthropologists, and the psychologists, and the Norse scholars, and the Scandinavian scholars, and the runic scholars, and even

Fig. 15. An undated photograph of Professor Ole Hagen. Courtesy of Janell Hagen Samuelson.

the occasional English professor like me. For better or worse, all of us are responsible for continuing Holand's work of maintaining the runestone's relevancy, though I'd argue the jury's still out on whether we're any closer to a conclusion.

Yet the strangeness of this story extends beyond the authenticity question. For me, equally odd is the stone's seemingly uncanny ability to adversely affect the reputations of so many who've dared to study it. Scholarly back-and-forth is to be expected, of course, though I know of few subjects that have prompted such controversy and animosity within a scholarly community.

Exhibit A: Dr. Olson's charges again Ole Hagen.

Do I believe Ole Hagen forged the Kensington Runestone's inscription?

I do not. Though Hagen may have possessed the runic knowledge that Olof Ohman lacked, I believe his moral fortitude would have prohibited him from such an act. It's a conclusion I've reached based on recreating his life as best I can by way of letters, photos, and stories of those who knew him or knew of him. Moreover, despite Dr. Olson's best attempt to peg Hagen to the scene of the crime, he was never able to do so. Finally, I just don't see a motive. What would possess an early-career, rising-star academic to concoct a scheme sure to inflict pain within his own scholarly community?

Dr. Olson had his theory. According to him, Hagen may have been inclined to commit such an act out of "contempt for American scholarship."

"He may have perpetuated the fraud to see what Scandinavian and other scholars would do with such a document," Dr. Olson suggested. He further insinuated that such a hoax might've been retribution for Hagen's failure to obtain the Scandinavian languages professorship at the University of Wisconsin, which Dr. Olson himself had received.

It's one theory. But to my mind, the notion that an academic—disgruntled or otherwise—would travel hundreds of miles to inscribe runes onto a stone for the sole purpose of sowing unrest seems nearly as strange as the prospect that fourteenth-century Norse explorers roamed west central Minnesota.

To turn the tables, what might've been Dr. Olson's motive to level charges against Hagen? For one, Dr. Olson sincerely believed he'd found his man. But did it run deeper than that? Did conflicting personalities play a role? After all, Dr. Olson and Hagen were classmates during their time in Madison. What we know of their relationship comes courtesy of Dr. Olson's letters, one of which offers insight on his feelings toward Hagen.

"When he was a student here he was looked upon as a learned fool," Dr. Olson wrote to a friend in 1910. "The year after his graduation, he remained here, and always walked about with a pair of black kid gloves on, and carried a cane. When the students met him, they took off their hats to him, but he does not seem to have understood that they were making fun of him."

Such a description hardly implies guilt. In fact, when I read these words over a century later, guilt is the last thing I think. Hagen was misunderstood, maybe. Different, perhaps. But such characterizations hardly make him a hoaxer.

*

An hour or so before arriving at the Runestone Museum, I continued west for another twenty miles until arriving at the site of the Ohman farm, known today as Kensington Runestone Park. After winding my way through the park entrance, I came to the exact plot of land from which the runestone was pulled. Standing on the slight hill, I tried to replay the 1898 scene in my mind: Olof manning the winch as he uprooted the aspen, the runestone at last visible. And the way the curiosity seekers soon flocked to his land, anxious to find what other secrets might be buried in the dirt.

I breathed in the crisp, fall Kensington air and imagined Norse explorers doing the same 655 years before. But did they? Did they camp not far from this spot, and then, after returning from a day of fishing, discover the bodies of ten of their men? The answer, of course, continues to be maybe but maybe not.

Which is the answer to most of the strange phenomena in this book. Maybe Lori Endrizzi saw the Beast of Bray Road, but maybe she didn't. Maybe Joe Simonton feasted on pancakes from outer space, but perhaps not, too.

Yet for me, the Kensington Runestone story is different from the ones that have come before. Primarily because this story seems a bit more personal. True enough, if authenticated, the runestone would further revise our understanding of North America's discovery, but in addition to that, it would also clear the names of several men decades after their deaths. Both outcomes would be important. After all, setting the record straight is setting the record straight—no matter how large or small.

*

Days after reading Dr. Olson's charges against Hagen, I come upon another stone. Not a runestone, but a gravestone, one whose etchings I can easily translate:

PROF

OLE E. HAGEN

1850–1927

This particular stone possesses its own mystery, claiming Hagen's birth year to be 1850, though other sources point to 1854. It's just one more tangle of history, one more question mark to add to the others. Yet more curious than Hagen's birth-year conundrum is the stone's reference to "Prof," even though, at the time of his death, he hadn't been a practicing professor in nearly two decades. Which to me, speaks to the pride he surely felt at having been one. And perhaps the regret, too, of not serving in that capacity longer than he had.

As a professor myself—one who teaches just miles from Hagen's former homestead—I understand the complications of the profession that both giveth and taketh away. I understand, too, the frustration of dedicating years of one's life to a subject of little interest to anyone. Some scholars, such as Hjalmar Holand, committed their lives to doubling down on an issue again and again. And some, like Ole Hagen, clung tight to their beliefs even when there was a price to be paid for it.

And for what?

Validation?

Vindication?

A handshake and a clap on the back?

I wonder what reception I'll receive for my own foray into this subject. I wonder, too, if I'm willing to risk as much as Hagen had.

Driving back to Eau Claire later that day, I'm struck by an unexpected realization.

How strange that the story of a man I never met somehow became my story, too.

*

Today, few people in and around Eau Claire remember the name Ole Hagen. One major exception is his granddaughter, Janell Hagen Samuelson, whom I meet in a local restaurant just days after seeing the stone. She's come bearing a bag full of family keepsakes: photographs, scrapbooks, even her grandfather's research pass to the British Museum.

"And here he is," she says, placing before me a black and white photo of Hagen. "I love this picture," Janell comments. "I love the bright look in his eyes, you know?" The light is, indeed, there. Of the many photos of Hagen I'll see that day, surely this one allows that light to shine the brightest. It depicts Hagen as a young scholar, not yet world-weary, and with his future stretched wondrously before him. A pocket-watch chain peeks from his inner pocket as his right hand rests atop a pair of books alongside a bowler cap.

"He was a man of impeccable character," Janell tells me, and as proof, recounts various stories in which he helped his extended family financially. When money was needed for medical costs or music lessons, Ole Hagen always came through as best he could. Such generosity extended to his livestock, too.

"His cows loved him," Janell tells me. "They'd follow him all around the yard. And when he moved them from the east side of Rock Falls to the pasture on the west side of town, they'd follow him the whole way"—a distance of six to eight miles, she estimates.

Every photo Janell shares offers me a glimpse into Hagen's life: there he is entertaining friends in Vermillion, giving English lessons to immigrants, and leaning across the table toward his infant son, Leif, in his highchair.

Yet for me, the most striking photo depicts a middle-aged, mustachioed Hagen staring directly at the camera, his eyes no longer retaining the light.

"You're welcome to keep that," Janell says as I hold the photo in my hands.

"You sure?"

She nods. "They made duplicates of everything."

Of the pictures, perhaps, but certainly not of Hagen's scholarship.

"Had the fire not occurred, it's possible we might know far more about the runestone today," I tell her.

"It's a shame," she agrees. All she knows of her grandfather's views on the runestone came by way of her father, who never said anything to discredit its authenticity.

"He never said that his father said anything negative about it either," she added.

The more I share regarding Dr. Olson's charges against her grandfather, the more Janell appears hurt by the blows leveled against her grandfather's reputation. No matter that a century has passed; for Janell, the wounds are fresh.

Janell concedes that though her grandfather may have possessed the knowledge to pull off such a hoax, "his character was such that it never would have committed him to do that."

While the Professor of Rock Falls was happy to engage with locals on conversations as wide-ranging as Latin prefixes and Assyrian translations, he was equally happy to lend a hand with a herd or offer firewood to a neighbor in need.

"Your academic pursuits are not the only thing you have contact with people about," Janell reminds me.

What is Hagen's story? Was he an innocent victim of the Kensington Runestone? A man in the wrong place at the wrong time with the right knowledge? Or was he, as Dr. Olson believed, the one responsible for perpetrating the alleged hoax?

Ole Hagen's life was much larger than a stone, and his contributions much greater than the controversy that surrounded him. The same is true of Hjalmar Holand, who had a full life beyond his crusade on behalf of the runestone. I imagine it's equally true for the others ensnared in this tale as well: Dr. Julius Olson, Olof Ohman, and so many more. Yet despite the richness of these lives, we remember these men most for their professional legacies—not necessarily "who they were" but "what they did."

Throughout my own quest to understand the Kensington Runestone, my interest in the stone itself has dissipated. For me, it's the men who matter most. Though I know that they, too, will always remain a mystery to me.

"My dad had a little saying," Janell says, offering me a glimpse of her father, "'a man convinced against his will is of the same opinion still.'"

I smile at the sentiment, one that simultaneously speaks to Hagen's refusal to refute the runestone's authenticity, as well as Dr. Olson's refusal to drop his case against Hagen. Both men held firm, though neither belief was popular.

"I wonder if his father taught him that," I say, mindful that Ole Hagen was a difficult man to convince.

"It's possible," Janell agrees.

Because, of course, anything is—no matter how strange.

Thanks to Hagen, as my journey winds down, I hit upon a lesson I hadn't yet considered:

When you dig deep enough for long enough, you always dredge up something.

What you choose to do with your find—how you interpret it—therein lies the mystery.

Epilogue

And So Concludes My Year of Living Strangely

One day while flipping through junk mail, I come upon a large, yellow envelope with my name written across its center. A glance at the return address confirms that I've at last received what I've been waiting for: a package of documents from longtime UFO logist Dr. A. R. Underwood.

For months Dr. Underwood and I had exchanged a series of phone calls, one of which concluded with his generous offer to send me information from his case files.

I told him I'd be happy to receive it.

And I was.

Tearing open the envelope, I begin with the letter written directly to me.

"I am enclosing excerpts from a private document, which I prepared in 2001, and circulated at that time to relatives and friends at that time, and summarized what I knew about UFOs in the late 1960's and early 1970's, when I looked into the matter at the time."

What follows is precisely that: five or so handwritten pages and schematics, as well as a few photocopies of previously published articles. The pages detail several specific UFO cases, but of most interest to me is Underwood's introduction, which provided insight into his personal experience as a UFO researcher.

"For a wide variety of reasons, chief among them a desire to know the truth, I decided in 1964 to take a serious, in-depth look at the UFO phenomenon. I did so despite being a young disciplinary chemist in the early stages of his professional career. And thus, I realized that such an interdisciplinary, controversial investigation could result in negative as well as positive personal and professional consequences."

As he soon learned, the majority of those personal and professional consequences proved to be negative.

Nevertheless, for years he continued the research, toiling away at the seemingly impenetrable subject.

To my mind, that's admirable, though to others, it surely seemed foolhardy.

After all, what good is the work if the work never reaches its end?

Researcher be warned: when it comes to the strange, the work never reaches its end.

Thankfully, for as long as there have been mysteries, there have been people willing to dedicate their lives to solving them. Often for no pay, little esteem, and no guarantee of an answer.

At the beginning of my year of "living strangely," I asked myself whether I could be one of them. If I was willing to purchase a wall full of filing cabinets, then dedicate the rest of my life to filling them with all things pertaining to the strange.

A year removed from that question, I can now say, unequivocally, that I am unwilling to do so. I've seen what commitment looks like, and I do not possess it. It's not that my interest in the strange has waned. If anything, it's heightened. But I now know that I'm simply not equipped to tackle every oddity the world has to offer. Even the Midwest proved too much for me.

Which is why, at journey's end, I've traded in my investigator's badge for my front row seat as a spectator to the investigations. It turns out I'm better at reporting the stories than solving them.

This is another way of saying that I've been humbled into acknowledging the things I don't know, won't know, and very likely can't know. That was the idea all along, of course—to embrace the strange wholeheartedly.

But I now know the downside of doing so: when you embrace the strange too tightly there's a chance it embraces you back.

*

Days when I find myself feeling frustrated by the world's many mysteries, I turn to the words of H. P. Lovecraft: "The most merciful thing in the world, I think, is the inability of the human mind to correlate all its contents."

Despite our brain's best efforts to fit every fact into the proper "envelope," it seems we're always a couple envelopes short.

Which makes sense given all that we don't know.

But the one thing I do know is that not every UFO sighting can be attributed to swamp gas or plasma or ball lightning. And not every sea monster is just some sea-monster-looking log. If indeed "stranger" explanations exist, then the only way we'll discover them is if we demonstrate a good faith effort in doing so. The same holds true for the more rooted-in-fact weirdness, such as the Hodag, Project ELF, and the Kensington Runestone. With these stories, we can at least confirm a few facts beyond a reasonable doubt. They've all fallen victim to various interpretations and spins, but at least they offer a bit of solid ground to stand on.

Though the strange remains as elusive as ever, I can take some satisfaction in having drawn at least a few conclusions.

First and foremost, I now have a much better understanding of the people who propagate the strange: who they are, what they think, and why. Having interviewed dozens, I believe that the majority of people who are fascinated by strange phenomena come at the subject from a place of curious inquiry. That is, they have no intention to mislead. Which doesn't mean they haven't occasionally been misled themselves. And by perpetuating the misinformation, they may have inadvertently misled others. Trust me, I am acutely aware of this problem and my place within it.

It's a tricky business, knowing who to trust. Because when we get it wrong—when we hitch ourselves to the wrong wagons—we expose ourselves to risk. In this field, one devoid of so much hard evidence, credibility is the only currency that matters. And once you spend it, you never fully get it back. This is the fear that keeps me fact-checking, even though I know full well that no fact-check will ever confirm everything. Especially when our facts are reliant upon humans. Time and again, when I asked my interviewees how they knew what information to trust, they always offered the same answer: they trusted the information if they trusted the person dispensing it. It's an imperfect system, but it's the same system we use in other aspects of our lives: from where we get our news to how we pick our plumbers. If we trust a source, we trust what that source has to say. Right up until that trust is compromised.

One last thought on the people who've committed themselves to the strange. Maybe it's a coincidence, or a result of the relatively small sample, but for whatever reason, the vast majority of the folks I've interviewed are products of the baby boomer generation. It's possible I was drawn to these people due to their lifetimes' worth of accumulated research, but I wonder, too, if culture and history play a role. When it comes to the UFO phenomenon, the majority of these folks grew up in the "golden age" of UFOs. Many folks I've spoken with agree that the UFO sightings of the 1950s and 1960s left their indelible mark. That these people were often interested in phenomena that I've classified as "Monsters" and "The Weird" is also worth pointing out. Were these folks embracing the strange in an effort to avoid confronting their own strange realities? Did these mysteries serve as welcome distractions from the darker concerns of the mid-twentieth century? After all, compared to the prospect of nuclear war, alien invasions, Hodags, and giant turtles must have seemed like quite a relief.

A second conclusion I've drawn is related to the tangible benefits available to communities that choose to embrace their own strangeness. Towns like Churubusco, Indiana; Point Pleasant, West Virginia; and Rhinelander, Wisconsin, have all been remarkably savvy in marketing their monsters, and to a lucrative end. Their annual festivals serve as proof; each of which fills motel rooms and restaurants in their respective towns. In addition to the potential for monetary gain, often these creatures serve as a source of town pride as well. More than a few folks informed me that their monster helped them earn a "dot on the map," giving their towns newfound importance and relevancy to the outside world. Every town needs its story, after all, and all the better if that story happens to be strange.

Finally, a third conclusion pertains to the subject of truth; in particular, how in some ways it has become ever more elusive over time. Which seems a mind-boggling claim given the seemingly endless supply of information most twenty-first-century citizens now have access to. But therein lies our problem: access to "more information" does not mean access to *better information*. In fact, the glut of "facts" is precisely what makes it so difficult to confirm much of anything. Every fact has its counter fact, every truth its counter truth. There's no "for better or worse" about it. For worse, we've reached a point in human history where muddying clarity has become big business, where swapping facts for fiction is its own cottage industry. In all that muck, it's no wonder we get sucked into it, if not swallowed up entirely.

*

One night—as my brain overflowed with runic symbols, Martian pancakes, and turtles as big as Buicks—I took refuge in my usual place: the kitchen pantry. I reached for a box of Celestial Seasonings tea and, lo and behold, there on the side of the box was the answer I'd been looking for.

No, not the answer to *all* the world's strangeness, but a clue as to why we often believe in it.

It was a quote from Ralph Waldo Emerson:

"We are born believing. A man bears beliefs as a tree bears apples."

Which, to me, speaks to two points. First, that we possess an innate desire to believe; that we are "born," as Emerson notes, leaning toward some tendency to fashion our belief systems. And second, that these belief systems grow—and become apparent to others—over time. That is, we are a product of our beliefs, and we have a hard time hiding that.

Maybe it's all as simple as recognizing that how we view the world is a matter of how we *choose* to view it. That one person's strange is another person's normal, and that what's weird to one is not necessarily weird to all.

Case in point: Does it seem weird to you that after a year's worth of weirdness, I'm taking my cues from quotations on tea boxes?

For me, it's not so weird, just further confirmation of my final finding:

That of the many strange things in our world, we humans remain the strangest of all. How else to explain our behavior? How we can be so fickle yet so stubborn? So certain in the face of uncertainty. So loyal to nothing more than a hunch.

Our quest to explore the world's mysteries is only natural, yet what's less natural—or at least less logical—are the ways in which many of us choose to explore. Not with curious inquiry, but a conqueror's spirit. When we approach mysteries merely as problems to be solved and questions to be answered, we lose sight of the larger reward: the mystery itself.

"It's okay not to be sure," astronomer Carl Sagan remarked in his essay "The Burden of Skepticism." Yet despite Sagan's permission, it sure doesn't feel okay. In a world that rewards answers, why settle for anything else? Later in the essay, Sagan urged humankind to strive to achieve an "exquisite balance," one that demands "the most skeptical scrutiny of all hypotheses" while also championing "a great openness to new ideas."

In short, we must be willing to think. Not to parrot what we've been told, but to employ our powers of deduction to examine information and, from it, draw a conclusion. Such an idea hardly seems revolutionary. The problem, Sagan explained, is that we no longer teach people *how* to think. "This is a very serious failure that may even, in a world rigged with 60,000 nuclear weapons, compromise the human future," Sagan concluded.

For those who struggle to understand the "usefulness" of exploring the strange, might I suggest examining it through Sagan's lens of human survival.

I'll be the first to admit that Bigfoot's existence (or not) is hardly the most pressing question of our time. Far more important is what Bigfoot—and all the other so-called monsters, Martians, and weirdness—have come to represent: our commitment to a good mystery.

The unanswered question, however, is whether we of the twenty-first century are willing to explore such mysteries in good faith. Can we be trusted to employ reason, logic, and critical thinking to reach a fact-driven conclusion? On our best days, perhaps. Though on the other days, it's a whole lot easier to go with our snap judgments instead. And our judgments, at least within the realm of this subject, are often the ones that offer us the least ridicule.

I'd like to tell you that I can personally confirm the existence of the Beast of Bray Road, Oscar the Giant Turtle, and Mothman. I'd like to tell you, too, that I solved the mysteries of those UFOs, bagged me a Hodag, and cracked the code of the runestone—all without breaking a sweat.

But the truth is, these days, truth is a whole lot harder to come by. And even when you think you know it, there's likely some fact out there to confirm that you don't.

Which doesn't mean we shouldn't keep tromping the woods in search of the strange, or focusing our eyes on that ripple in the water. But let's not limit our search to those terrains. And let's remember, too, that we're best served by beginning all our searches with a good, hard look in the mirror.

As we take that good, hard look, we might also ask *why* we believe strange things. What, specifically, compels us to believe that which we cannot prove? Is it our love for a good story? Or our fear of having figured everything out?

There's no one answer. As confirmation bias confirms, we humans simply have a tendency to see what we want to see and believe what we want to believe. Equally troubling is the alacrity with which we're willing to dispense with everything that fails to fit within our preferred version of truth.

I'm as guilty as anyone.

Only now—after a year of "living strangely"—am I beginning to recognize the ways in which I let my own preferred version of truth take priority over the truest version. The mind is a powerful thing, but so is the heart. We must all confront how we balance our facts with our faith.

Reader, as we come to the end of our journey, I regret to inform you

Fig. 16. The author and his children in search of the "strange." Courtesy of the author.

that there's no one key to unlock the world's mysteries. Thankfully, not all mysteries require such treatment. Perhaps the key we're really after unlocks a more personal mystery: how to live our lives to ensure that neither science nor imagination are deemed liabilities. Better still if we view their convergence as a strength.

No matter what you believe, here's one truth we can all agree on:

We humans—with all our complexities—are surely the crown jewel in any cabinet of curiosities.

Embrace it.

We are who we are.

Our greatest mystery is our capacity for wonder.

SOURCES

This book was written from various sources, including firsthand accounts, scholarly research, and online and newspaper articles. What follows is the list of sources I most heavily relied upon while crafting individual chapters. The sources are ordered approximately according to the information's placement within each chapter. If a source was employed multiple times throughout the chapter, I listed it only upon its initial use. In reference to "Case File #5: The Minot Air Force Base Sighting," unless otherwise indicated, all quotations are from the many linked resources and interviews available on Thomas Tulien's online compendium, "A Narrative of UFO Events at Minot Air Force Base."

PROLOGUE: MY YEAR OF LIVING STRANGELY
Holars, *In Defense*; Keel, *The Mothman*.

CASE FILE #1: THE BEAST OF BRAY ROAD
Godfrey, *Beast*; Godfrey, "Tracking"; Godfrey, "I Never"; "History"; Olshefski, "Carson's"; Godfrey interview; "Confirmation Bias"; "Gray Wolf"; "Gray Wolf Recovery"; Schackelman interview; Coleman, "Gable"; Boese, *The Museum*; Lamb interview; Linshi, "Here's"; Polden, "I Want"; Watson, Chaneles, and Lee, "Golden."

CASE FILE #2: OSCAR THE TURTLE
Gutowski, *American*; Doran, *The Hunt*; Harris, "The Beast"; Mathieu interviews; Jones interviews; "Here's How"; "1949 Turtle Hunt Log"; Mathieu, "Oscar"; Smith, "Marjorie Courtenay-Latimer"; Gutowski interview; Wilson interview.

CASE FILE #3: MOTHMAN
"Couples See"; O'Neill, "Welcome"; Siler, "Mason Countians"; Wamsley interview; Turner, "Mason Bird"; Brook, "Inside"; Slowik, "Chicago's Mothman";

Strickler, "Chicago Owlman"; Strickler, "Bat"; Strickler, "Large"; Strickler interview; Godfrey interview; Strickler, "Chicago Phantom"; Keel, *The Mothman*; Walkinshaw, "Migration"; "Strange Plane"; LeRose, "The Collapse"; Casale, "4 Alleged"; Bennett, "Monster"; Turner, "Mason Bird"; "Giant Owl"; Nickell, "'Mothman.'"

CASE FILE #4: JOE SIMONTON'S SPACE PANCAKES
Simonton, *The Story*; Carter, "Judge"; "Got 'Cakes'"; Sontag, "The Imagination"; Center, "Eagle River"; Clark interview; Jung, *Flying*; Hynek, *The UFO*; Clark, "The Pancakes"; Carter interview.

CASE FILE #5: THE MINOT AIR FORCE BASE SIGHTING
Tulien, "A Narrative"; McNeff interview; Ward, "UFO Network"; Tulien interview; O'Connell, *The Close*; Denzler, *The Lure*; "End of the U.F.O. Hunt"; Lyons, "Air Force"; Isley interview.

CASE FILE #6: THE VAL JOHNSON INCIDENT
Johnson interview; Kruglanski, Webster, and Bjork, "Motivated"; Paranormal, "That's Incredible"; Mezrich, *The 37th*; Pappalardo, "Declassified"; "List of"; "319th Air Base Wing"; Beitman, "Brains"; Ackerman, "I Sing"; "'UFO Squad Car'"; Miller, "Philip"; Klass, *UFOs*; Longdon, "Philip."

CASE FILE #7: THE HODAG
Kortenhof, *Long Live*; Kearney, *The Hodag*; Shepard interview; Olsen, *Our First*; Shidell interview; Gard and Sorden, *Wisconsin*; Shepard, "Boost."

CASE FILE #8: PROJECT ELF
"Independence Day"; "Operation"; "Convention"; Hertzel, "A Message"; Klessig and Strite, *The ELF*; Klessig, "Papers"; Clam Lake; Rice interview; Reinders interview; Biasi interview; Claus et al., *Project*.

CASE FILE #9: THE KENSINGTON RUNESTONE
Blegen, *The Kensington*; Holand, *Norse*; Krueger, "A Viking"; Wahlgren, *Kensington*; Hjalmar and Harold Holand, Papers; Olson, Papers; Cummins, *The University*; Holand, "Concerning"; Samuelson interview.

EPILOGUE: AND SO CONCLUDES MY YEAR OF LIVING STRANGELY
Underwood, Personal communication; Sagan, "The Burden."

SELECTED BIBLIOGRAPHY

Please find below a list of referenced sources. This list is not exhaustive, but rather, the sources that proved most pertinent to this book.

Ackerman, Diane. "I Sing the Body's Pattern Recognition Machine." *New York Times*. June 15, 2004. http://www.nytimes.com/2004/06/15/science/essay-i -sing-the-body-s-pattern-recognition-machine.html?_r=0.

Anderson, Rasmus B. *America Not Discovered By Columbus*. Madison wi: Leif Erickson Memorial Association, 1930.

Associated Press. "Close Encounter Makes Him Famous." *Kingman Daily Miner*, September 10, 1979.

——— . "Monster Bird With Red Eyes May Be Crane." *Gettysburg Times*, December 1, 1966.

"Avro Canada vz-9 Avrocar." Wikipedia, the Free Encyclopedia, last modified October 1, 2018. https://en.wikipedia.org/wiki/Avro_Canada_VZ-9_Avrocar.

Beitman, Bernard D. "Brains Seek Patterns in Coincidences." *Psychiatric Annals* 39, no. 5 (2009): 255–64.

Bennett, Roger. "Monster No Joke For Those Who Saw It." *Athens Messenger*, November 18, 1966.

Biasi, Tom. Interview with author, August 24, 2017.

"'Birdman' Could Be fhs Balloon." *Huntington Herald-Dispatch*, November 18, 1966.

Blegen, Theodore C. *The Kensington Runestone: New Light on an Old Riddle*. St. Paul mn: Minnesota Historical Society, 1968.

——— . "O. E. Hagen, a Pioneer Norwegian-American Scholar." In *The Immigration of Ideas*, edited by J. Iverne Dowie and J. Thomas Tredway, 43–65. Rock Island il: Augustana Historical Society, 1968.

Boese, Alex. *The Museum of Hoaxes: A History of Outrageous Pranks and Deceptions*. New York: Plume, 2002.

Brook, Pete. "Inside the Eerie TNT Storage Bunkers of West Virginia." *WIRED*, March 31, 2014. https://www.wired.com/2014/03/joshua-dudley-greer-tnt -storage/.

Brooks, Maurice. *A Check-List of West Virginia Birds*. Bulletin 316. Morgantown WV: Agricultural Experiment Station, 1944.

"Busco's Behemoth Turtle Roams Lake." *Fort Wayne Journal Gazette*, March 10, 1949.

Carlozo, Lou. "The Ongoing Mystery of Indiana's Sasquatch in a Shell." *Chicago Tribune*, June 26, 2002.

Carter, Colyn. Interview with author, August 6, 2017.

Carter, Franklin. "Judge Avers Story True." *Saucerian Bulletin* 6, no. 1 (December 31, 1961): 2–6. http://www.cufos.org/Saucerian/1961_12_31_Saucerian_Bulletin _Vol-6%231(W%2324).pdf.

Casale, Steven. "4 Alleged Mothman Sightings That Preceded Disasters." *The Portalist*, August 17, 2017. https://theportalist.com/4-alleged-mothman-sightings -that-preceded-disasters.

Center for UFO Studies. "Eagle River, WI 1961." http://www.cufos.org/cases/1961 _04_18_US_WI_Eagle-River_HYNEK_Simonton-CE-III.pdf/.

Clam Lake: Elk Capitol of Wisconsin. http://clamlakewi.com/.

Clark, Jerome. Interview with author, July 18, 2017.

———. "The Pancakes of Eagle River." *International UFO Reporter* (Spring 1996): 3–8.

Claus, Eric, et al. *Project ELF Oral History Project, 1994–1999*. Madison WI: Wisconsin Historical Society Archives.

Coleman, Loren. "Gable Film Returns: Werewolves on MQ Finale." *Cryptozoonews*, March 22, 2010. http://www.cryptozoonews.com/gable-film-returns/.

"Confirmation Bias." Wikipedia, the Free Encyclopedia, last modified October 2, 2018. https://en.wikipedia.org/wiki/Confirmation_bias.

"Convention on the Prohibition of Military or Any Other Hostile Use of Environmental Modification Techniques," U.S. Department of State, May 18, 1977. https://web .archive.org/web/20070914081350/http://www.state.gov/t/ac/trt/4783.htm.

"Couples See Man-Sized Bird . . . Creature . . . Something." *Point Pleasant Register*, November 16, 1966.

Cummins, Cedric. *The University of South Dakota: 1862–1966*. Vermillion SD: Dakota Press, 1975.

Denzler, Brenda. *The Lure of the Edge: Scientific Passions, Religious Beliefs, and the Pursuit of UFOs*. Berkeley CA: University of California Press, 2003.

Doran, Terry, dir. *The Hunt for Oscar*. 1994. https://www.youtube.com/watch?v =cW5IW9KfqsQ.

———. "Pursuit of the 'Beast of Busco . . .'" In *Turtle Days, 1974*, 8, 14, 38. Churubusco IN, 1974.

"End of the U.F.O. Hunt." *New York Times*, December 19, 1969.

Gard, Robert Edward, and L. G. Sorden. *Wisconsin Lore*. New York: Duell, Sloan and Pearce, 1962.

"Giant Owl Killed on Area Farm." *Point Pleasant Register*, December 22, 1966.

Godfrey, Linda. *American Monsters: A History of Monster Lore, Legends, and Sightings in America*. New York: Tarcher, 2014.

———. *The Beast of Bray Road: Tailing Wisconsin's Werewolf*. Black Earth WI: Prairie Oak Press, 2003.

———. "I Hope This Doesn't All Start Up Again." *The Week*, May 10, 1992.

———. "I Never Dreamed I'd Be Famous—For THIS!" *The Week*, January 12, 1992.

———. Interview with author, June 19, 2017.

———. *The Michigan Dogman: Werewolves and Other Unknown Canines across the USA*. Eau Claire WI: Unexplained Research Publishing Group, 2010.

———. *Monsters among Us: An Exploration of Otherworldly Bigfoots, Wolfmen, Portals, Phantoms, and Odd Phenomena*. New York: TarcherPerigee, 2016.

———. *Real Wolfmen: True Encounters in Modern America*. New York: Jeremy P. Tarcher, 2012.

———. "Tracking Down 'The Beast of Bray Road.'" *The Week*, December 29, 1991.

"Got 'Cakes' from Saucer Men Is Claim of Joe Simonton." *Vilas County News-Review*, April 27, 1961.

"Gray Wolf Fact Sheet." Wisconsin Department of Natural Resources, 2017. http://dnr.wi.gov/topic/wildlifehabitat/wolf/facts.html.

"Gray Wolf Recovery in Minnesota, Wisconsin, and Michigan." U.S. Fish and Wildlife Service, 2011. https://www.fws.gov/midwest/wolf/aboutwolves/r3wolfrec.htm.

Gutowski, John. "American Folklore and the Modern American Community Festival: A Case Study of Turtle Days in Churubusco, Indiana." PhD diss., Indiana University, 1977.

———. Interview with author, May 9, 2017.

Hancock, Peter. *Hoax Springs Eternal: The Psychology of Cognitive Deception*. Cambridge: Cambridge University Press, 2014.

Harris, Helen. "The 'Beast of Busco.'" In *Turtle Days, 1974*, 1. Churubusco IN: 1974.

"Here's How Churubusco Got Its Name." *Churubusco Truth*, August 1, 1963.

Hertzel, Leo J. "A Message from Clam Lake." *North American Review* 266, no. 2 (June 1981): 9–18.

"History." Elkhorn Area Chamber of Commerce & Tourism Center, Inc., 2014. http://www.elkhornchamber.com/pages/History.

Holand, Hjalmar R. "Concerning the Kensington Rune Stone." *Minnesota History* 17, no. 2 (1936): 166–88. http://collections.mnhs.org/MNHistoryMagazine/articles/17/v17i01p020-037.pdf.

———. *Norse Discoveries and Explorations in America: 982–1362; Leif Erickson to the Kensington Stone*. New York: Dover, 1940.

Holand, Hjalmar Rued, and Harold Holand. Hjalmar and Harold Holand Papers, 1922–1972. Green Bay WI: University of Wisconsin–Green Bay Archives and Area Research Center.

Hollars, B.J. *In Defense of Monsters*. Durham: Bull City Press, 2017.

Hynek, J. Allen. *The Hynek UFO Report*. New York: Dell, 1977.

———. *The UFO Experience: A Scientific Inquiry*. Chicago: Henry Regnery, 1972.

Hynek, J. Allen, and Jacques Vallee. *The Edge of Reality: A Progress Report on Unidentified Flying Objects*. Chicago: Henry Regnery, 1975.

"Independence Day 1977 Downbursts." National Weather Service. https://www.weather.gov/grb/070477_downburst.

Isley, Lloyd. Interview with author, June 16, 2017.

Johnson, Val. Interview with author, January 12, 2017.

Jones, Chuck. Interviews with author, July 14, 2011, and June 30, 2016.

Jung, C. G. *Flying Saucers: A Modern Myth of Things Seen in the Sky*. London: Routledge, 2002.

Kearney, Lake Shore. *The Hodag and Other Tales of the Logging Camps*. Wausau WI: Democratic, 1928.

Keel, John A. *The Mothman Prophecies*. New York: Tor, 1991.

Klass, Philip J. *UFOs: The Public Deceived*. New York: Prometheus Books, 1983.

Klessig, Lowell L. Papers, 1969–1982. Madison WI: Wisconsin Historical Society Archives.

Klessig, Lowell L., and Victor Strite. *The ELF Odyssey: National Security Versus Environmental Protection*. Boulder CO: Westview Press, 1980.

Klose, Kevin. "Navy Begins Building of Controversial Radio Station." *Washington Post*, December 25, 1983. https://www.washingtonpost.com/archive/politics/1983/12/25/navy-begins-building-of-controversial-radio-station/a7bf2c2b-fcbf-4881-8403-459a983ec57a/?utm_term=.abe5413d67ea.

Knoll, Erwin. "The Navy in the North Woods." *The Progressive*, October 1969.

Kortenhof, Kurt Daniel. *Long Live the Hodag! Timber Cruiser, City Booster and Practical Prankster: The Life and Legacy of Eugene Simeon Shepard, 1854–1923*. Master's thesis, University of Wisconsin–Eau Claire, 1996.

Krueger, David. *Myths of the Runestone: Viking Martyrs and the Birthplace of America*. Minneapolis: University of Minnesota Press, 2015.

———. "A Viking Myth at the Smithsonian?" Myths of the Runestone, posted June 10, 2016. https://mythsoftherunestone.com/tag/hjalmar-holand/.

Kruglanski, Arie W., Donna M. Webster, and Robert A. Bjork. "Motivated

Closing of the Mind: 'Seizing' and 'Freezing.'" *Psychological Review* 103, no. 2 (1996): 263–83.

Lamb, Jess. Interview with author, June 19, 2017.

Landsverk, O. G. *Ancient Norse Messages on American Stones*. Glendale CA: Norseman Press, 1969.

Laycock, George. "Not All Is Sanguine in Wisconsin." *Audubon*, January 1970.

LeRose, Chris. "The Collapse of the Silver Bridge." *West Virginia Historical Society Quarterly* 15, no. 4 (October 2001).

Linshi, Jack. "Here's the World's Fastest Dog on Two Paws." *Time*, August 27, 2014. http://time.com/3195860/jiff-worlds-fastest-dog/.

"List of X-Planes." Wikipedia, the Free Encyclopedia, last modified July 24, 2018. https://en.wikipedia.org/wiki/List_of_X-planes.

Longdon, Tom. "Philip Klass." *Des Moines Register*, May 27, 2005. http://data.desmoinesregister.com/famous-iowans/philip-klass.

Lyons, Richard D. "Air Force Closes Study of U.F.O.'s." *New York Times*, December 18, 1969.

"Mason County Has 'Flying' Mystery." *Morgantown Dominion*, November 18, 1965.

Mathieu, Chuck. Interviews with author, July 14, 2011, and June 30, 2016.

———. "Oscar, Myth or Reality . . . and Why It Was Good for Churubusco." In *60th Anniversary of the Hunt for Oscar*, 2–3. Churubusco IN, 2005.

McNeff, Bill. Interview with author, January 19, 2017.

Mezrich, Ben. *The 37th Parallel: The Secret Truth Behind America's UFO Highway*. New York: Atria Books, 2016.

Miller, Stephen. "Philip Klass, 85, Journalist Debunked UFO Reports." *New York Sun*, August 12, 2005. http://www.nysun.com/obituaries/philip-klass-85-journalist-debunked-ufo-reports/18507/.

Nickell, Joe. "'Mothman' Solved!" *Skeptical Inquirer*, March/April 2002.

"1949 Turtle Hunt Log." In *60th Anniversary of the Hunt for Oscar*, 9–11. 2009.

O'Connell, Mark. *The Close Encounters Man: How One Man Made the World Believe in UFOs*. New York: Dey Street Books, 2017.

Olsen, T. V. *Our First Hundred Years: A History of Rhinelander*. Rhinelander WI: PineView Press, 1981.

———. *Rhinelander Country Volume Two: Birth of a City*. Rhinelander WI: PineView Press, 1983.

Olshefski, Kellen. "Carson's Christmas Card Features Iconic Sprague Theater." MyWalworthCounty.com, November 13, 2014. http://mywalworthcounty.com/?p=12023.

Olson, Julius E. Julius E. Olson Papers, 1894–1938. Madison WI: Wisconsin Historical Society.

O'Neill, Claire. "Welcome to the 'TNT Area,' Home of the Mothman." The Picture Show: Photos from NPR, January 23, 2012. https://www.npr.org/sections /pictureshow/2012/01/23/145334460/welcome-to-the-tnt-area-home-of-the -mothman.

"Operation Popeye." Wikipedia, the Free Encyclopedia, last modified on September 12, 2018. https://en.wikipedia.org/wiki/Operation_Popeye.

Pappalardo, Joe. "Declassified: America's Secret Flying Saucer." *Popular Mechanics*, February 11, 2013. http://www.popularmechanics.com/military/a8699 /declassified-americas-secret-flying-saucer-15075926/.

Paranormal Videos You May Have Missed. "That's Incredible!—Val Johnson Case." YouTube, November 4, 2015. https://www.youtube.com/watch?v=lFs3nrFfnxo.

Peterson, Victor. "They've Lassoed Gale Harris' Turtle!" *Indianapolis Times*, July 10, 1949.

Pliny the Elder. *The Natural History*, ed. John Bostock and H. T. Riley. London: Taylor and Francis, 1855. http://data.perseus.org/citations/urn:cts:latinLit: phi0978.phi001.perseus-eng1:1.dedication.

Pohl, Frederic J. *The Viking Explorers*. New York: Thomas Y. Crowell, 1966.

Polden, Jake. "I Want To Walk Like You! Unbelievable Moment Bear Stands on Their Hind Legs Like Humans and Even Run Alongside Tourist Bus as They Beg for Food," *Daily Mail*, April 15, 2016. http://www.dailymail.co.uk/news /article-3541419/I-want-walk-like-Unbelievable-moment-bears-stand-hind -legs-like-humans-run-alongsidetourist-bus-beg-food.html.

Reinders, Pat. Interview with author, August 24, 2017.

Rice, Lynne. Interview with author, August 24, 2017.

Sagan, Carl. "The Burden of Skepticism." *Skeptical Inquirer* 12 (Fall 1987): 1–13. https://www.scribd.com/document/24763842/Carl-Sagan-The-Burden-of -Skepticism.

Samuelson, Janell Hagen. Interviews with author, September 29, 2017, and October 5, 2017.

Sandberg, Walt. "Code Name: Sanguine." *Wisconsin Sportsmen* 2, no. 1 (December/ January 1973):40–41, 53.

"Saucer Story Is Set for TV Report." *Vilas County News-Review*, May 11, 1961.

Schackelman, Joe. Interview with author, June 27, 2017.

Shepard, Eugene. "Boost Northern Wisconsin." *New North*, November 28, 1907.

Shepard, Eugene, and Karetta Gunderson Shepard. *Paul Bunyan: His Camp and Wife*. Tomahawk WI: Osborne Press, 1929.

Shepard, Layton. Interview with Dave Peterson and L. G. Sorden, September 30, 1963. Madison WI: Wisconsin Historical Society Archives.

Shermer, Michael. *Why People Believe Weird Things: Pseudoscience, Superstitions, and Other Confusions of Our Time*. New York: Holt, 2002.

Shidell, Jerry. Interview with author, March 20, 2017.

Siler, Pat. "Mason Countians Hunt 'Moth Man.'" *Huntington Herald-Dispatch*, November 17, 1966.

Simonton, Joe. *The Story of the Flying Saucer: As It Was Seen By Joe Simonton*. Eagle River WI, 1961.

"Simonton Reports More Unidentified Flying Objects Here." *Vilas County News-Review*, August 10, 1961.

Slowik, Ted. "Chicago's Mothman Stories Are Good Paranormal Entertainment." *Chicago Tribune*, July 29, 2017. http://www.chicagotribune.com/suburbs /daily-southtown/opinion/ct-sta-slowik-chicago-mothman-st-0730-20170728 -story.html.

Smith, Anthony. "Marjorie Courtenay-Latimer." *The Guardian*, May 20, 2004. https://www.theguardian.com/news/2004/may/21/guardianobituaries.

Sontag, Susan. "The Imagination of Disaster." In *Against Interpretation, and Other Essays*, 209–25. New York: Farrar, Straus and Giroux, 1966.

"Strange Plane Turns Out to Be a Bird." *Point Pleasant Register*, December 5, 1966.

Strickler, Lon. "'Bat out of Hell' Witnessed by Father and Son—Little Calumet River in Chicago." *Phantoms & Monsters* (blog), April 30, 2017. http://www .phantomsandmonsters.com/2017/04/breaking-bat-out-of-hell-witnessed -by.html.

———. "Chicago Owlman/Mothman Seen Again By Multiple Witnesses!" *Phantoms & Monsters* (blog), August 18, 2017. http://www.phantomsandmonsters.com /2017/04/chicago-owlman-mothman-seen-again-by.html.

———. "Chicago Phantom Leaps from Willis Tower." *Phantoms & Monsters* (blog), July 24, 2017. https://www.phantomsandmonsters.com/2017/07/chicago -phantom-leaps-from-willis-tower.html.

———. Interview with author, September 12, 2017.

———. "Large Winged Humanoid Encountered Again in Lincoln Park, Chicago." *Phantoms & Monsters* (blog), June 4, 2017. http://www.phantomsandmonsters .com/2017/06/large-winged-humanoid-encountered-again.html.

"319th Air Base Wing." Wikipedia, the Free Encyclopedia, last modified May 12, 2018. https://en.wikipedia.org/wiki/319th_Air_Base_Wing.

Tulien, Thomas. Interview with author. June 6, 2017.

———. "A Narrative of UFO Events at Minot Air Force Base." October 24, 1968: Minot AFB, North Dakota. Sign Oral History Project. 2017. http://minotb52ufo.com/.

Turner, Ralph. "Mason Bird Monster Presumed Gone Now." *Huntington Herald-Dispatch*, November 22, 1966.

———. "That Mothman: Would You Believe a Sandhill Crane?" *Huntington Herald-Dispatch*, November 19, 1966.

"Turtle Doomed—Farmer to Drain Lake." In *Turtle Days, 1974*, 37. Churubusco IN, 1974.

"'UFO Squad Car' Still a Talker at Minnesota County Fair." *Pioneer Press*, July 24, 2013. http://www.twincities.com/2013/07/24/ufo-squad-car-still-a-talker-at-minnesota-county-fair/.

Underwood, Dr. A. R. Personal communication, August 27, 2017.

Wahlgren, Erik. *The Kensington Stone: A Mystery Solved*. Madison: University of Wisconsin Press, 1958.

Walkinshaw, Lawrence H. "Migration of the Sandhill Crane East of the Mississippi River." *Wilson Bulletin* 72, no. 4 (December 1960): 358–84.

Wamsley, Jeff. Interview with author, October 13, 2017.

Ward, Bill. "UFO Network Members Are Down to Earth." *Star Tribune*, October 5, 2011. http://www.startribune.com/ufo-network-members-are-down-to-earth/131164383/.

Watson, Jane Werner, Sol Chaneles, and Alan Lee. *The Golden Book of the Mysterious*. New York: Golden Press, 1976.

Wayland, Tobias. "Insect-Like Flying Humanoid Reported on Chicago's Willis Tower." Singular Fortean Society. 24 July 2017. https://www.singularfortean.com/news/2017/7/24/insect-like-flying-humanoid-reported-on-chicagos-willis-tower?rq=willis%20tower.

Wilson, Miles. Interview with author, June 30, 2016.